The Teacher and the Teenage Brain

T0353023

The Teacher and the Teenage Brain is essential reading for all teachers and students of education. This book offers a fascinating introduction to teenage brain development and shows how this knowledge has changed the way we understand young people. It provides a critical insight into strategies for improving relationships in the classroom and helping both adults and teenagers cope better with this stage of life.

Dr John Coleman shows how teachers and students can contribute to healthy brain development. The book includes information about memory and learning, as well as guidance on motivation and the management of stress. Underpinned by his extensive work with schools, Dr Coleman offers advice on key topics including the importance of sleep, the social brain, moodiness, risk and risk-taking, and the role of hormones. This book is extensively illustrated with examples from classrooms and interviews with teachers. It explicitly links research and practice to create a comprehensive, accessible guide to new knowledge about teenage brain development and its importance for education.

Accompanied by a website providing resources for running workshops with teachers and parents, as well as an outline of a lesson plan for students, *The Teacher and the Teenage Brain* offers an innovative approach to the understanding of the teenage brain. This book represents an important contribution to teacher training and the enhancement of learning in the classroom.

Dr John Coleman trained as a clinical psychologist and was formerly a Senior Research Fellow at the University of Oxford. He is the founder of a research centre studying adolescents and their families, and during his career he has also run a special school for troubled teenagers and worked as a policy advisor for government. In addition to running workshops for parents of teenagers, he has created two series for TV, and written books and developed videos on the adolescent years. John's pioneering work has been widely recognised, and in the Queen's Birthday Honours in 2001 he was awarded an OBE for services to young people.

The Teacher and the Teenage Brain

John Coleman

Routledge
Taylor & Francis Group

LONDON AND NEW YORK

First published 2021
by Routledge
2 Park Square, Milton Park, Abingdon, Oxon OX14 4RN

and by Routledge
52 Vanderbilt Avenue, New York, NY 10017

Routledge is an imprint of the Taylor & Francis Group, an informa business

British Library Cataloguing-in-Publication Data
A catalogue record for this book is available from the British Library

Library of Congress Cataloging-in-Publication Data
Names: Coleman, John C. (John Christopher), 1940- author.
Title: The teacher and the teen brain / John Coleman.
Description: Milton Park, Abingdon, Oxon; New York, NY: Routledge, 2021. |
Includes bibliographical references and index. |
Identifiers: LCCN 2020053869 (print) | LCCN 2020053870 (ebook) |
ISBN 9780367435790 (hardback) | ISBN 9780367435813 (paperback) |
ISBN 9781003004462 (ebook)
Subjects: LCSH: Adolescent psychology. | Teenagers–Education. |
Teacher-student relationships.
Classification: LCC BF724 .C56 2021 (print) | LCC BF724 (ebook) |
DDC 305.235/5–dc23
LC record available at https://lccn.loc.gov/2020053869
LC ebook record available at https://lccn.loc.gov/2020053870

ISBN: 978-0-367-43579-0 (hbk)
ISBN: 978-0-367-43581-3 (pbk)
ISBN: 978-1-003-00446-2 (ebk)

Typeset in Sabon
by Deanta Global Publishing Servies, Chennai, India

Access the companion website: www.routledge.com/cw/coleman

Contents

Acknowledgements

A project of this sort is bound to be a collaboration between many different people, and I am hugely grateful to all who made this work possible. First and foremost, I must mention the team in Hertfordshire who had the idea in the first place. Special thanks to David Silverman, Joella Scott, Lucy Sims and Breda O'Neill whose enthusiasm and commitment kept the work going over a number of years.

None of it would have happened without the involvement of the staff at Family Links, a remarkable organization based in Oxford. Their involvement in the project, and their skills as trainers, have been integral to the project. It has been a great pleasure working with Sarah Darton, Kathy Peto and Rowen Smith.

The team at the Early Help service in Bedford Borough saw the potential of this work for parents of teenagers, and their support enabled me to develop a workshop for this group. I would like to express my thanks to Chris Morris, Chris Allan, Chris Lee and all the other trainers at the Early Help service.

Many schools showed an interest in the work and allowed me to try out early versions of the lesson plan with their students. I should particularly like to mention Sylvia Jennings at Presdales School in Ware, Louise Reynard at Broxbourne School, Katie Southall at Priory School in Hatfield and Debi Roberts who made it possible for me to work at Sandringham School in St Albans. All these teachers contributed their ideas in interviews and helped me unstintingly.

Other teachers agreed to take part in a telephone interview about the teenage brain, including Sophie Antwi of Chancellors School, Paul Marlow of Hertswood Academy, Chris Allan of Bedford Borough, Beatrice Fairclough-Adamson of Hertswood Academy and Rosemary Inskip of Kings School, Langley. Thanks to all of them for their contributions.

As the work progressed, I began to develop a model for "Training the trainers". Many organizations have shown in interest in this work, and I would particularly like to mention the Charlie Waller Trust, Parenting Northern Ireland and Hertfordshire Children's Services. All these have supported further work to enable more trainers to develop the confidence to deliver workshops on the teenage brain.

I would like to mention the Association for Young People's Health, my professional home during the course of this work. To all the wonderful people at AYPH – thanks for your interest and support.

This has been a time of remarkable progress in our understanding of the teenage brain. New research findings are appearing all the time, and many people have written about this topic in the last few years. I am especially grateful to Sarah Jayne Blakemore in this respect. We met a few times during the course of my work, and she has always been both interested and supportive. Her own book, *Inventing ourselves: The secret life of the teenage brain*, won the 2020 British Psychological Society Book Prize, an honour as well as a recognition that the neuroscience of adolescence has come of age.

In addition to the work of Sarah Jayne, I have learnt an enormous amount from those in education and neuroscience who have been publishing books on this subject while I have been developing my ideas and trying out better ways to make this knowledge accessible. I would particularly like to pay tribute to Paul Howard Jones, Frances Jensen, Eveline Crone, Michael Thomas, and Adriana Galvan. They are the pioneers, and their work has been invaluable for me in the course of my own learning.

I wish to dedicate this book to all the teachers, young people, parents and practitioners who were willing to act as guinea pigs in this ground-breaking project. Thank you to all of them.

John Coleman
November 2020

Chapter 1

Ten things every teacher needs to know about the teenage brain

This is a book for teachers, but what can teachers gain by learning about the teenage brain? How will this subject assist teachers in their work? In the process of writing this book, I have asked many teachers what it is about the teenage brain that they would like to know. I have had many different answers, but one teacher got to the heart of things by asking:

"Can you tell me how to engage the reasoning side of a teen's brain?"

This is a great question – a two-pronged question. At first, it appears to refer to logical thinking. It seems to concern the rational part of the brain. How can we improve the young person's ability to solve problems, to reason, to engage in scientific thinking?

However, on second thoughts, there is something else here. The question could be asking about the awareness of consequences. How can we stop teenagers behaving thoughtlessly? The question raises the idea of a "reasoning side" of the brain as opposed to the emotional side of the brain. What does this mean? Where does it reside? How can we best facilitate it and support its development?

Other teachers asked a wide range of questions. Here are just a few.

- "Can knowing about the brain help me motivate my students?"
- "Is there such a thing as left-brain thinking?"
- "How to get through to an individual who is in a heightened emotional state?"
- "At what age does the fear factor kick in, so that they understand consequences?"
- "Is it really true that the brain shrinks during the teenage years? How can this be?"

There has been a lot of debate about whether neuroscience – the science behind brain development – can actually lead to more effective teaching and learning. My answer to this is a categorical YES! Knowing about the brain will not answer all teachers' questions. It will not address everything you need to know about teaching. It may not necessarily help you with lesson planning, curriculum design or the use of technology in the classroom.

It will, however, make a profound difference to your teaching. The reason for this is that knowledge about the brain during the teenage years has altered the way we understand young people. It has given us new insight into their development during these critical years.

- Did you know that the teenage brain is especially responsive to rewards?
- Did you know that the brain matures from back to front?
- Did you know that the grey matter in the brain does actually reduce by about 17% during this stage?
- Did you know that memory processes are active during sleep, thus contributing to learning during the day?

If you are interested in these questions, and many others – read on. However, just before we get to my first of ten things – "A thing of wonder" – I want to outline the structure of this book. In this first chapter, I will describe ten ideas concerning the brain. This is a short introduction to some key concepts, many of which will be explored in greater detail later in the book. There will then be a chapter on other aspects of teenage development, and this will be followed by a description of my journey from thinking about the baby's brain to considering the teenage brain.

Next will come a series of chapters detailing some major areas of research, including learning and memory, the social brain, sleep and so on. Finally, at the end of the book you will find three chapters with a more practical slant. Here I discuss the development of workshops and training on the teenage brain for teachers, students and parents. These chapters outline the background and activities that have made it possible for me to create these learning materials. More detail about the workshops can be found in Appendix 2 and the accompanying website (www.routledge.com/cw/coleman).

One last point. This book has been written during the pandemic of 2020–21. It is hard to know what the long-term impact will be on young people and on their lives in the future. I will refer to the pandemic in Chapters 2 and 8. At this stage we can only guess at how education, employment, health and social life will be impacted in the future. No matter how challenging and stressful the experiences of these years, young people will continue to change and develop. I know that the information in this book, describing the development of the brain during the teenage years, will remain relevant to teachers and to all who live and work with young people.

1. A thing of wonder

The human brain is a wonder and a mystery. It is a thing of magic, yet it is a concrete object. It is extraordinary – the most complex thing you can imagine. There is nothing in nature that has any parallel. Today, science is beginning to unravel a tiny fraction of the mystery, but only a tiny fraction.

To begin with the brain contains billions of cells, known as neurons. Your brain contains perhaps 80 or possibly 100 billion neurons. More than all the stars in the galaxy, more than the entire global population, more than the human brain can comprehend.

How is it possible to make sense of such an organism? It is of such complexity, yet weighs less than three pounds, and is something that you could easily hold in your hands.

All these billions of neurons are connected to other neurons in patterns and networks. We still understand very little about how these networks function, and how the multitudes and multitudes of neurons work together in systems to ensure that humans walk, talk, learn, memorise and collaborate together in social groups.

The brain operates by sending messages along pathways between neurons. Each neuron has branches that connect to other neurons. A neuron sends messages to other neurons by passing an electrical current, or impulse, along these branches. Remarkably, there is a tiny gap in the middle of each branch, known as the synapse. The message, the impulse, has to jump over this gap in order to reach the next neuron. There will be more about this in a minute.

I will now turn to the structure of the brain. During the teenage years, three areas are especially important. One is the prefrontal cortex, associated with thinking, reasoning, problem-solving and other intellectual activities. The second is the amygdala, an area buried deep in the brain and associated with emotion, sensation and reward-seeking. The third is the hippocampus, the area most associated with

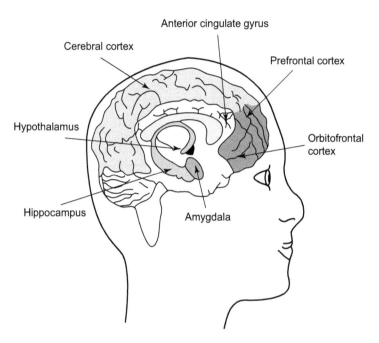

Anterior cingulate gyrus

Cerebral cortex

Prefrontal cortex

Hypothalamus

Orbitofrontal cortex

Hippocampus

Amygdala

Figure 1.1 Simplified image of the structure of the brain, showing the pre-frontal cortex, the amygdala and the hippocampus.

memory processes. These areas of the brain undergo major development and change at this time. You can see where these are located in Figure 1.1.

The last 20 years have seen a giant leap forwards in our understanding of the human brain. This is because of the development of scanning technology. It is now possible to take pictures of the brain as it functions, without any great distress or discomfort. The technology is known as magnetic resonance imaging.

The development of brain imaging has provided amazing insights into the teenage brain. However, I have called this section "A thing of wonder" for a reason. Scanning can only tell us so much. Scanning allows us to see how much oxygen is going to different parts of the brain at any one time, which is a huge advance on what was possible 20 years ago. Nonetheless, this is still very limited. In the next sections, I will describe what we have learnt about the teenage brain. In the last section of the chapter, I will discuss what adults can do to assist with healthy brain development during the teenage years.

2. How the brain works

As I have said, the brain is enormously complex. While it is not necessary for a general reader to understand too much of the technical stuff, it is useful to have some basic knowledge about the brain and how it works. I will try and make this section as simple as possible.

I will start with neurons. Each neuron has branches that connect to other neurons. One branch is called the axon, while others are called dendrites. For each neuron, there is one axon, but many dendrites. A pulse, or signal, is sent out by the neuron, it travels along the axon, crosses the synapse and connects to a dendrite on the other side that takes it on to the next neuron. It is hard to comprehend, but this is happening millions of times in your brain during the course of any one second (Figure 1.2).

The synapses play a central part in the story, as they can be seen as the on/off mechanism in the brain. Within the synapse are what are known as chemical messengers (or neurotransmitters). These are hormones that either help or hinder the transmission of neural messages. Synapses are designed to act as either facilitators or inhibitors of further travel of an impulse.

This is hugely important because there are simply too many stimuli entering the brain at any one time. The brain needs a filter mechanism. Without such a mechanism you would not be able to concentrate or pay attention, as you would be constantly distracted by other messages

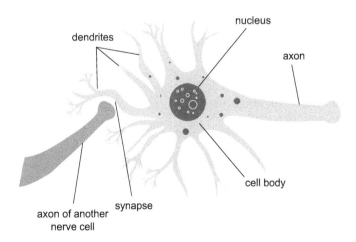

Figure 1.2 Image of a neuron, showing axon, dendrites and synapse.

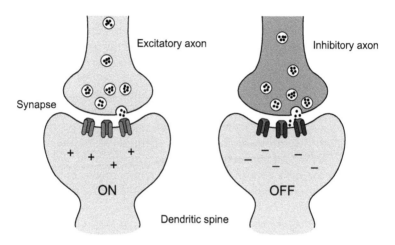

Figure 1.3 Image of two types of receptor.

arriving in the brain. Some people like to say that the synapses are the air traffic control system for the brain, preventing constant mid-air collisions! (Figure 1.3).

In addition, myelin is important. This is the substance that covers the axon, and it has two purposes. First, it helps speed up the transmission of a message. This is significant in adolescence, as the myelin around the axons increases in size during this stage, allowing faster transmission of signals from one part of the brain to another. Myelin also plays a big role in helping to keep the neurons, axons and dendrites separate from each other. You may be able to imagine what a tangle of connections there must be in such an extraordinarily small space in your brain. The myelin helps to keep things apart and function effectively.

It is now time to think about what makes the teenage years special as far as brain development is concerned.

3. What is special about the teenage years?

It is a remarkable fact that it is only in the last 20 years that we have learnt how much change occurs in the brain during the teenage years. Previously, it had been assumed that the brain had matured by the end of childhood. Now, as a result of studies using scanning technology, we understand that the teenage years are a period when the brain alters more than at any other time apart from the first three years of life.

This is important because a time of such change is a critical period. The experiences that a young person has at this stage will affect brain development to a greater extent than at other times in life. It is for this reason that the more teachers and other adults understand what is happening to the teenage brain, the better it is for healthy adolescent development.

This is the period when the brain goes through a major process of maturation. It becomes more efficient, and a variety of new skills and abilities develop. Memory, language, thinking and reasoning all improve. How does this happen?

I have already mentioned the change in the thickness of the myelin around the axon. This change allows impulses to travel around the brain in a faster and more efficient manner. In addition, all areas of the brain mature, and this applies especially to the three key areas of the brain I have already mentioned: the prefrontal cortex, the amygdala and the hippocampus. These areas do not necessarily mature at the same rate. As a general rule, it can be said that the brain matures from back to front, with the prefrontal cortex being the last to become fully mature.

In order to understand how we measure maturation, I need to point out that the brain is in two halves, two hemispheres as they are known (Figure 1.4). As a result, the two sides of the brain have to work together. How do they do that? They are connected by a bridge,

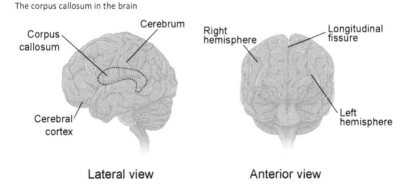

The corpus callosum in the brain

Corpus callosum

Cerebrum

Cerebral cortex

Right hemisphere

Longitudinal fissure

Left hemisphere

Lateral view   Anterior view

Figure 1.4 Image showing two hemispheres of the brain, with the bridge (the corpus callosum) in the middle.

but you can imagine how much traffic that bridge has to carry if the two halves of the brain are to function effectively. A key change that takes place at this time is a maturation of this bridge, allowing the connections to increase and become more varied. This assists the young person to develop new neural pathways and to draw upon more areas of the brain when thinking and reasoning. We call this element of brain function connectivity. As connectivity increases, so the brain becomes more efficient and skilful.

The fascinating thing about this process of increased connectivity is that it does not occur in a uniform way across the brain. So, when I said that the brain matures from back to front, I could have said that the increasing connectivity starts in the back of the brain – in the area to do with physical activity – and gradually moves forward towards the prefrontal cortex.

This is a central fact in understanding the teenage brain. The difference in rates of maturation in different parts of the brain is sometimes used to explain risky or thoughtless behaviour. I shall have more to say about this later.

One other key aspect of the teenage brain has to do with white and grey matter. The grey matter lies on the outside of the brain and is where most of the neurons exist. The white matter is in the centre and is where most of the connections between neurons occur.

You will remember that I mentioned earlier that some parts of the brain shrink during this period. Let me explain. One very important aspect of brain development at this stage is that there is a major increase in grey matter in late childhood. This mainly happens just before puberty. However, this increase leads to the brain having too many neurons and synapses.

As a result, during the next few years there is a process known as pruning. Gradually, the unwanted connections are allowed to die away, while the useful connections become reinforced. This process is a fundamental part of brain development, allowing useful connections to thrive and removing connections that serve no purpose. You may have heard the phrase "use it or lose it". This refers to the pruning process.

Scientists have shown that there is a 17% reduction in grey matter over this period. I cannot emphasise enough how significant this is. In order for this to be achieved the brain has to undergo a major reorganization and restructuring. It is no wonder then that young people experience times of uncertainty and confusion (Figure 1.5).

How moody teenagers are (literally) losing their mind

David Sanderson Arts Correspondent

Teenagers are unfairly demonised by a society that is just beginning to study the enormous loss of grey matter in their brains during adolescence, according to a leading neuroscientist.

Sarah-Jayne Blakemore said that moodiness, risk-taking, sleepiness and embarrassment at parents should be sympathised with and understood in the context of the changes in the adolescent brain.

MRI studies showed that between childhood and adulthood the brain underwent a substantial "pruning" of its synapses and an "enormous" 17 per cent reduction in grey matter in the pre-frontal cortex, she said.

The professor of cognitive neuroscience at UCL added that the education system should be altered to take the changes into account. She advocated allowing later starts to the school day to help circadian rhythms, or the biological clock, and an appreciation of the "Key Stage 3 dip" when the educational performance of children falls between the ages of 11 and 14. Professor Blakemore said that rather than teenagers being mocked for their moodiness, laziness and recklessness parents should speak to them about the changes.

She told the Hay Festival that teenage behaviour had been put down to sex hormones, puberty and changes such as starting secondary school. "The teenage brain is not broken, it is not dysfunctional, it is not a defective adult brain; it is a formative period in life where the brain is changing in really important ways where neural pathways are malleable and passion and creativity run high," said Professor Blakemore, whose book *The Secret Life of the Teenage Brain* brings together the latest studies. "We should not demonise this period of life we should understand it, nurture it and celebrate it."

She said it was impossible for scientists to judge the impact of technology on the younger brain, and added that concerns about social media should not detract from other teenage stresses.

Figure 1.5 Article from the *Times* newspaper. © The Times/ News Licensing. Originally published 30 May, 2018.

Because this is a time of such major change, the environment around the young person is especially important. This means that key adults, such as teachers, have a big role to play in assisting healthy brain development. This may appear fanciful. While we know that adults can make a difference to things like health and learning, we do not pay much attention to the brain, as it is invisible and has until recently been largely unknowable.

Now that we are learning more about the brain, however, we are beginning to discover that there are experiences that assist brain development, and experiences that are not so helpful. A look at the different hormones in the brain will help to explain this in greater detail.

4. The role of hormones in the brain

We all know something about hormones, probably because of sex hormones such as oestrogen and testosterone. The levels of these hormones increase at puberty, and they have a profound effect on our sexual development and sexual behaviour. In addition to these hormones, there are dozens of other hormones that affect the way the brain functions. There are a few that are particularly important in relation to the teenage years, and I will outline these shortly.

First, however, we should recognise that the teenage years are often linked with an upset of the hormone balance. Adolescence is sometimes described as being a time when "hormones are all over the place". We can see this in common behaviours such as mood swings and the flip-flop of emotions.

One of the things we have learnt as a result of research on the teenage brain is that there is a marked level of variation in the hormone balance in this age group. All of us have some degree of daily variation in the balance of hormones in our brains. The variation for teenagers, however, is much greater than for other age groups. Thus, the level of any of the key hormones may be going up and down to a significant extent during any 24-hour period. It is not surprising then that this affects behaviour and means that at times emotion regulation can be hard for young people.

Let us now look at some of the most important hormones. Serotonin is a hormone that is released when we feel good, happy, relaxed and at ease. This is the hormone that helps keep our mood steady. Low levels of serotonin can be a factor in depression. Variation in serotonin levels may play a part in leaving teenagers at the mercy of feelings of sadness or misery. Young people who have extreme reactions to minor setbacks ("What's the point? I might as well give up right now!") may be experiencing significant variation in levels of serotonin.

Cortisol is one of the major hormones released when we are anxious, stressed or vulnerable. On a short-term basis, cortisol can be useful. When we are under threat it is the hormone that prepares our body to respond appropriately. This is the famous "fight or flight" response. However, too much cortisol has a detrimental effect on our bodies and leads to poor functioning. There will be more about this in Chapter 8 on stress and mental health.

Two other hormones are useful to know about. One is melatonin, and I will discuss this later when I cover the topic of sleep. The second hormone that is important to mention is dopamine. You may have heard people speak of something called a "dopamine rush". Dopamine is known as the reward hormone, the hormone that is released when an individual gets pleasure, a reward or a thrill.

We now know that there are more dopamine receptors in the teenage brain than in brains of people of other ages. This means that dopamine is an especially active hormone during these years. This can lead to a sensitivity to rewards, as well as a motivation to seek rewards. There will be more about this later in the book.

5. Risk-taking and reward-seeking

The mention of the hormone dopamine is a helpful lead-in to a discussion of risk-taking and reward-seeking. There are two aspects of brain development that may play a part here. In the first place, there is the possible difference in the rate of maturation between the thinking part of the brain, the prefrontal cortex, and the emotional part of the brain, the amygdala.

I noted earlier that the brain matures from back to front. This means that the amygdala, part of the limbic system in the central area of the brain, may mature earlier than the prefrontal cortex. In the first wave of research reports (say from 2000 to 2010), it was often suggested that "a developmental mismatch" occurred in the teenage brain, leading to risk-taking behaviour. This was because the behaviour was more likely to be governed by the need for sensation or reward, rather than by cognitive control.

In recent years, scientists have become cautious about this, as more research evidence has become available. This "developmental mismatch" may be true of some individuals, or it may be true on some occasions, but it is probably not the case for everyone all the time.

The second possible reason for risk-taking and reward-seeking has to do with the hormone balance in the brain at any one time. In the previous section I mentioned dopamine. For some young people, at some points in time, higher levels of dopamine may lead to a push for rewards and exciting experiences. At these times, the prefrontal cortex is less effective at controlling behaviour. We all know young people who, when asked why they did something apparently senseless, respond by saying: "I just didn't think".

One other factor to be taken into account is that the brain is undergoing an enormous amount of change. As a result, there will inevitably be a period of adjustment. It may not be easy to be sensible and mature on every occasion. If adults instinctively feel critical of young people, it is helpful just to remember how much is happening in the brain at this time.

When thinking about reward-seeking and risk-taking, it is important to keep in mind the role of the environment. The brain is clearly very important, but there is an interaction between brain and environment. The family context and the role models available to the young person play a part. It is also relevant to consider social pressures, as they too exert an influence on these less than positive behaviours.

The role of the peer group offers a good example of this. Research clearly shows that during this stage young people are more likely to take risks or to respond impulsively, if they are with peers, rather than on their own. Young people appear to be more affected by peer group influences than adults. This is an illustration of the role played by social factors in risk-taking behaviour. The brain plays its part, but it does not act in isolation from the environment.

6. New skills

When thinking about the teenage brain there is a tendency to empha-sise the enormous change that takes place. This encourages us to think about the difficulties that the young person faces at a time of such major adjustment. However, there is another side to the story. This is also a time when very positive things are happening. Important areas of the brain are maturing, allowing new skills to develop.

In the first place, the areas and networks in the brain that are to do with memory and learning alternate to allow new thinking and an increased capacity. If we think for a moment about the changes in the curriculum in Key Stage 3 (ages 11 to 14), we can see that the teenager would not be able to manage all this new schoolwork without being able to draw on new capabilities. There needs to be some development in thought processes, as well as the ability to develop scientific reason-ing. During these years, the maths and science curriculum becomes more complex, and so new thinking skills are essential in order to cope with increasing intellectual demands in lessons.

Memory capacity is also advancing during these years. While this is not something that is routinely tested in school, research on memory has shown a marked change with age. As young people move through secondary school their memory develops in order to cope with the increasing demands made on them in tests and exams.

Of course, it is possible to train the memory, and no doubt experi-ences at school add to the increasing capacity. However, we also know that changes in the brain allow this process to happen more easily. We should note that the area of the brain most often associated with memory, namely the hippocampus, is one that has been identified as undergoing major change and maturation during the adolescent years.

Another new skill that develops during this period is language. At the beginning of the teenage years, an individual will have about 75% of an adult's vocabulary. During the years that follow, vocabulary will increase significantly, as will skills to do with communication.

Some readers may find this hard to comprehend because many teen-agers come across as either tongue-tied or unwilling to talk to adults. Nonetheless, communication skills will be maturing during the ado-lescent years as areas in the brain related to language go through a process of development. A teenager's unwillingness to communicate may be more to do with a dislike of being interrogated, or a need for privacy, than any failure of language development.

Thinking, language and memory are not the only skills develop-ing at this time. The young person is also developing a much greater awareness and concern with social relationships, and this increased concern is linked to other aspects of brain development. I will now turn to what is known as the social brain.

7. The social brain

As we have learnt more about the changes that are going on in the adolescent brain, we have understood that some of these changes take place in areas to do with social functioning. The term "social brain" refers to the regions that have to do with understanding other people. On the one hand, the development of the social brain leads to the development of new skills. On the other hand, some short-lived deficits make it difficult for the young person to see the wider picture. Some commentators have described teenagers as having "tunnel vision" for a period when they seem to be focussed more on themselves than on other people.

Looking first at the new skills that develop, these have to do with understanding the thoughts or intentions of others. These include being able to take the perspective of another person, understanding the mental states of others, identifying intentions and recognizing emotions. All these are useful as the young person becomes more involved with the peer group and with close friends. The development of these skills appears to be closely associated with the development of the prefrontal cortex and with other areas to do with thinking and cognition.

However, strangely, at the same time as this is happening, there are also moments when the ability to see another person's side of the story appears to desert the young person. Some writers have used the term "adolescent egocentrism" to describe this state. It is at this stage that the teenager becomes preoccupied with his or her own emotions and sees the world from one perspective only. It is likely that this feature of behaviour has a lot to do with increasing self-awareness, which is another aspect of the changes that are taking place at this time.

We should not be surprised that this all appears very contradictory. We might say: "How is the young person able to understand other people's perspectives at the same time as having a self-centred view of life?" However, this contradictory feature of the teenager's behaviour reflects exactly what is happening. Major structural change is taking place in the brain, and this cannot happen overnight. It takes time for all areas of the brain to function effectively together. There will be occasions when self-awareness will be developing alongside the growth of new social skills.

I will make one final point in relation to the social world. Research has shown that in neutral situations, adolescents have similar cognitive abilities and response times to adults. However, in stressful or emotional situations, young people are more open to influences from the peer group. There will be more about this in Chapter 6.

8. The question of sleep

One of the important findings that has come from work on the brain has to do with sleep in the teenage years. Most parents and carers will have noticed that at times teenagers appear unwilling to go to sleep, while at other times it is impossible to get them out of bed. Teachers may notice students being half-awake in the early part of the school day.

It is only in recent years that we have learnt why this happens. It is not, as was assumed, because young people just want to be contrary. There is a biological reason for the altered patterns of sleep in adolescence.

The hormone that makes us feel sleepy is melatonin. It is released in the brain at roughly the same time each night, signalling that it is time to go to bed. However, we have learnt that melatonin is released later in teenagers than it is in adults. This means that young people do not necessarily feel sleepy at the same time as others in the family and may find it more difficult to get to sleep.

Of course, melatonin is not the only factor that influences whether we feel sleepy or not. The amount of light is important, and what we eat and drink plays a part too. However, levels of melatonin do make a difference, and certainly have an influence on the sleep patterns of many teenagers.

This is significant because teenagers need their sleep. If adolescent sleep is monitored in a laboratory, young people will sleep for more than nine hours. And research also tells us that sleep deficit (having fewer than seven hours a night) can affect school performance as well as behaviour. It will be obvious that if a young person has to get up for school early in the morning, while at the same time having gone to sleep late at night, this will restrict the amount of sleep that is possible.

Over the last few years sleep has been the subject of many research studies. These studies have shown that sleep is not just for rest. A number of significant things happen during sleep, making it even more important for teenagers to get a good night's sleep.

During sleep:

- Growth hormones are released;
- Memory consolidation occurs, allowing the learning that has taken place in the day to be embedded in long-term memory;
- A cleaning-up process takes place, enabling the management and disposal of waste products produced in the brain during the day.

All this illustrates just how important sleep is for us all. Yet the group for whom this is most important is the group attending secondary school and further education. There will be much more detail about sleep in Chapter 7.

9. Vulnerable teenagers and the role of the brain

There are many ways in which young people can show that they are vulnerable. This may be through moods and emotions, through behaviour, through poor health or through troubled relationships. While I cannot cover all aspects of the topic in this brief section, I will mention a few mental health problems. In Chapter 8 it will be possible to explore these issues in more depth.

The main purpose of this section is to show how our knowledge of the brain can help us understand the mental health of young people. Attention deficit is a good place to start. You will remember that, in the brain, electrical impulses travel from one nerve cell to another by moving along the nerve fibre, jumping across the synapse and moving to the next neuron. This is happening millions of times in the brain at any one moment.

Clearly, the brain has to have the capacity to manage all these impulses, allowing some to travel on and shutting down others when they interfere or get in the way. This is the role of the chemical messengers, as they affect how the impulse crosses the synapse.

This may seem a very simplistic model of how the brain works, but in essence, this model enables us to understand something like attention deficit or impulsive behaviour. If for one reason or another the chemical messengers are not functioning effectively, the individual will feel bombarded with impulses and find it difficult to sort out which should be attended to and which should be ignored. A young person who cannot pay attention in class will be in exactly this position. A teenager who acts impulsively may do so because the brain is not being effective in connecting the planning and thinking regions with those that are to do with emotional reactions.

While it is important to note that there are different types of depression, some forms of mood disorder may be affected by the chemical balance in the brain. One type of depression arises because of external events such as trauma or loss, but another type of depression occurs without an obvious external cause. It is this type of depression that may be linked to hormones in the brain. If levels of serotonin, for example, are too low, this may lead to a slowing down of the travel of impulses, making the individual feel sad or disengaged.

Lastly, it is useful to look at anxiety. A chemical that I have not mentioned so far is the GABA neurotransmitter. This is a chemical messenger that plays a key role in reducing the excitability of neurons and thus helping to control anxiety or fear. Where GABA is too low, it may be more difficult to control unhelpful emotions. There are, of course, other chemical messengers involved in anxiety, but GABA is a very common one. Medications to reduce anxiety work to enhance the natural effects of GABA.

I must emphasise that many factors will create vulnerability in an individual. The brain is only one factor, acting in combination with what has happened to the young person in the past, and what is going on around them in the present. Thus, the environment can affect the brain, but what is happening in the brain may, in turn, influence the individual's behaviour, and therefore, on their environment.

10. Adults can make a difference

I have made it clear in this introductory chapter that major changes occur in the teenage brain, and these changes have a profound effect on behaviour and development. The changes are invisible, so it is easy to miss the fact that these developments are happening. In this section, I want to spell out how the adults around the teenager can make a difference to brain development.

The first thing is to do with understanding. Teenagers experience a major upheaval and readjustment of their brains. If they have teachers, parents or carers around them who understand this and take it into account, it can make a significant difference to general well-being. It is also important for adults to know that this is a critical period, and thus what happens at this time will have long-term implications. New patterns and pathways are being laid down, and new ways of thinking and managing emotions are developing. Experiences during this period actually matter for future development.

As one teacher put it to me after she had delivered a workshop on the brain to her colleagues:

> When I delivered it to all staff, they said it made them think differently. They were very positive about it. They said it made them think differently when young people presented with anxiety, or when pupils got frustrated, finding it difficult perhaps to focus. It made them think about doing shorter sharper activities, and about rewards and praise. How we can make sure that pupils are more engaged across the whole curriculum? It was all really helpful.

The second thing to keep in mind has to do with the role of chemical messengers in the brain. A good balance of different hormones is essential if the brain is to manage the process of pruning unwanted connections while developing and embedding useful neural pathways. If the young person experiences too much anxiety or stress, the hormone balance will hinder this fundamental process.

It is here that adults have such a vital role. On the one hand, they can make a difference in the environment surrounding the young person. The more supportive this is, the more likely it is that the hormone balance will facilitate positive growth and development. On the other hand, adults have a part to play in helping young people manage stress and anxiety. If the teenager can learn to manage these emotions, hormones such as cortisol will be kept to reasonable levels. However, high levels of a hormone such as cortisol will inhibit learning and make the management of emotion more problematic.

The next thing to mention relates to the role of the amygdala and the prefrontal cortex. You will remember that these two areas of the brain undergo rapid development, but there may be times when the amygdala plays a more powerful role than the prefrontal cortex. This would mean more emotion and less thinking, and therefore, a greater likelihood of reward-seeking or risk-taking behaviour.

For this reason, it is important to encourage the development of the prefrontal cortex, and here again, adults such as teachers and parents have a part to play. The more enriching the environment, and the wider range of activities the young person is engaged in, the more opportunities there will be for the prefrontal cortex to mature faster. In this way, behaviour is more likely to come under the control of the cognitive part of the brain, rather than being governed by the search for sensation and immediate reward.

I will give one last illustration of the role of adults. As I have explained, emotion regulation can be hard at this time. All aspects of brain development play into this. Different parts of the brain mature at different rates. Hormone variation has its effect, as well as the restructuring caused by pruning. All these things are easier to manage if the young person is helped to create good routines.

In the family, this applies to sleep, eating and other health-related issues. In school, this relates to timetabling, planning and revision for tests and exams. These things are sometimes known as study skills. If students can be helped to create routines for themselves around key educational tasks, this will be of enormous benefit in overcoming some of the challenges resulting from brain development.

In this introductory chapter I have given an overview of what we know about the teenage brain and I have set out how this knowledge can be of value to all engaged in education. All the topics covered here will be explored in greater detail in later chapters. It is now time to turn to Chapter 2, in which I will outline a different perspective on teenage development.

Further reading

Blakemore, S-J (2019) *"Inventing ourselves: The secret life of the teenage brain"*. Transworld Publishers/Penguin, London.

Crone, E (2017) *"The adolescent brain: Changes in learning, decision-making and social relations"*. Psychology Press/Routledge, Abingdon, Oxon.

Galvan, A (2017) *"The neuroscience of adolescence"*. Cambridge University Press, Cambridge.

Jensen, F (2015) *"The teenage brain: A neuroscientist's survival guide to raising adolescents and young adults"*. Harper, New York.

Chapter 2

A brief introduction to teenage development

Introduction

In Chapter 1, I outlined the key facts about brain development. This will help readers grasp the scale of the changes occurring in young people during this life stage. It is now time to look at other aspects of development so that readers can gain a more rounded picture of the teenager. How can we describe this period of life? This is often seen by adults as puzzling, contradictory and difficult to understand.

One of the questions I am frequently asked is: when do the teenage years begin, and when do they end? This is not an easy question to answer, as there are such large individual differences. As we shall see when I discuss puberty later in the chapter, this key event can occur at age 9 or 10, but it can also occur at 13 or 14. Thus, it will be evident that it is not easy to pinpoint the exact moment when the individual actually becomes a teenager.

It is even more complex at the other end of this stage. As social changes have impacted on those aged 18 and above, it becomes harder to achieve full adult status. More individuals remain in the family home for longer periods, and more find that their entry into the world of work is delayed.

One of the most interesting findings from brain research is that some of the changes I have outlined in Chapter 1 continue into the mid-twenties. This underlines the fact that development continues well after the actual term "teenager" can apply. In this book, I will be concentrating largely on those in the secondary school age range. Nonetheless, it is worth keeping in mind that the age group between 18 and 24, most often known as young adults, will experience continuing change. Simply because young people have left school does not mean that development has ceased.

In this chapter, I will argue that the teenage years should be considered as a transition, and I will look at the nature of transitions to provide a perspective on this stage. I will then go on to outline some aspects of social change that have a direct impact on teenage development. Following that, I will discuss a theory of human development that offers a valuable perspective on the teenage years. I will then consider puberty and its impact on development. This will be followed by some thoughts about parenting, and the chapter will conclude with a short reflection on vulnerability.

Transition

It is helpful to think of this stage as a major transition. This is a journey from childhood to maturity. Within the overall transition, there are, of course, many smaller transitions. There is the move from one school to another, the changing relationship with close adults, the possibility of the beginning of a sexual relationship, moving away from home and so on. The shift from being a child to being an adult is a long and complicated process. Because of this, the young person can be both mature and immature at the same time.

This is often reflected in behaviour. At one time the teenager will act as in an adult manner, taking decisions and managing day-to-day activities without adult involvement. However, at another time the young person will behave like a needy child, seeking help and guidance. This can be very frustrating for adults, but it is a natural part of the transition process.

The key element of a transition is uncertainty about whether you are in one state or the other. It is this uncertainty that helps to explain many of the behaviours that are typical of the teenage years. Transitions have a number of common characteristics. These include:

- An eager anticipation of the future (wanting to be grown-up)
- A sense of loss or regret for the stage that has been left behind (still showing childish behaviour or expressing childish needs)
- A sense of anxiety about what is unknown (worrying about the future)
- A major psychological readjustment (changes in all domains)
- A degree of ambiguity of status during the transition (no one knowing quite what status should be accorded to the young person during this stage).

These characteristics of the transitional state create a world of questions and challenges. As one parent put it: "You never know where you stand. One moment they're up, the next they're down". It is important to recognise that being "neither one thing nor the other" poses special difficulties for all concerned. Everyone wants to know where they stand and what is expected of them. Yet during the process of transition, this is not always possible. Teachers and parents are never quite sure how to treat the young person during these years. It is difficult for the adult to determine quite how much to expect of the teenager and how much autonomy to allow.

Transition is tricky for the young person too. What is reasonable to expect from the adults around you? One the one hand, the young person wants to be treated as a responsible person, but sometimes that can be scary. Being looked after and having things done for you can feel safe and comforting. Add to that the swings of emotion that young people experience almost daily, and we can see that transitions can be challenging for all concerned.

Social change

One factor that has a profound influence on the type of transition experienced by the young person is the social context in which they grow up. The world that surrounds the teenager today is very different from the world as it was in, say, 1970, or even in 1990. We should keep in mind that the teenager of today was born in the first decade of the 21st century, already very different from the 20th century. In this section, I will briefly explore some of the major changes that have occurred in the social world that are affecting the lives of young people.

There are a number of topics that might be considered under the heading of social change. The four most obvious ones are:

- The family
- The transition from education to employment
- Multi-culturalism
- The impact of the digital world.

This book is being written during the pandemic of 2020–2021. It is very difficult to say at this point how the first lockdown in the summer of 2020, and subsequent lockdowns, will affect young people. There are going to be long-term implications for their lives in the future, as far as education is concerned, but also for the economy, health and other factors at present impossible to foresee. Covid-19 cannot be ignored as a factor influencing the lives of this generation of young people. I will say more about the impact of the pandemic when discussing stress in Chapter 8.

Turning now to the family, this is something that continues to evolve and alter with time. Divorce is now widespread, and all teenagers will have had experience of family breakdown, even if it does not apply directly to their own family. Some teenagers live with parents who are not married, others live with lone parents, while others live in stepfamilies or blended families. On the one hand, it may be that the changing family has almost become the norm, yet, on the other hand, this has significant implications for young people. The parenting of teenagers is harder in these new family forms, so that vital support for young people may be lacking. Having restricted access to one parent who is no longer living at home can also impact on the well-being of a young person. Lastly, the uncertainties that come from a changing family create additional stresses at a time of life where stable support is essential.

It is well-known, and hardly has to be stated, that secondary education has experienced constant change in the 21st century. Alterations to the curriculum and in examination structures, as well as the increasing demands put on teachers, are all of great significance for young people. In addition, young people are staying on longer at school with the increased participation agenda, and there have been numerous changes in the provisions for 16- to 18-year-olds. Also, entry to the labour market has become more problematic, with major changes in employment opportunities for young adults. Writing today it is important to note that higher youth unemployment will be one of the consequences of the pandemic. This fact, combined with the changes mentioned here, are all going to impact on the life chances and the development of teenagers growing up.

The increase in ethnic diversity is another factor that contributes to a changing social context. The circumstances of those from diverse ethnicities are something that has been at the forefront of social and political discussions in recent times. While, on the one hand, more opportunities have opened up for those from BAME backgrounds, on the other hand, prejudice remains endemic in many walks of life. There are many ways that young people from a variety of cultural and ethnic backgrounds are playing a full role in society. However, the fact remains that the chances for those from such backgrounds are still far too limited. The experience of racism is damaging and distressing to those who have to live with this aspect of life in Britain. There is no doubt that the life chances of many from culturally diverse backgrounds are negatively influenced or restricted by racial prejudice. Higher rates of exclusion from school and entry into the criminal justice system for young Black men are just two instances of the way these attitudes play out for certain young people. It is to be hoped that, with more recognition of racism in society, it will be possible for the life chances of all young people from BAME backgrounds to improve.

Finally, in this section, some mention must be made of the digital world. The role played by social media in the lives of young people cannot be underestimated. The opportunities offered by the digital medium have changed the social context for teenagers growing up in this century. However, there are two points to be made here. Adults spend as much time online as do teenagers, so we have to be very careful not to assume that this is simply a teenage phenomenon. The second point is that online and offline worlds combine and interact, both being important in their own ways. Young people still want to see their friends and share real-world activities. It is essential to remember that the virtual world and the physical world work together.

Many aspects of the digital world give rise to adult anxiety. As readers will be only too well aware these threats include grooming, pornography, gaming and the possibility of addiction, online bullying and other worrying aspects of social media. Against that, however, it is essential to see the positive opportunities afforded by the digital world. The internet has changed so many aspects of life and has provided so many new avenues through which we can experience our social relationships. Life for a 21st-century teenager is unimaginable without being able to live in the virtual world just as easily as in the physical world. Most teenagers would say this has created a richer life.

Lifespan developmental theory

I will not spend too much time in this chapter on the theories of adolescence. However, I do think it is worthwhile to mention lifespan developmental theory, as it contributes a useful perspective on this stage. The theory applies to all life stages, but it has particular things to say about the teenage years. The theory emphasises five elements that affect human development. These are:

- Historical and geographical context
- Continuity
- Timing of life events
- Mutuality
- Agency.

Historical and geographical context

The first concept inherent in the lifespan development model has to do with **context**. This is sometimes referred to as historical time and place. The argument here is that all human development occurs in a particular context and that we need to take this into account if we wish to understand a particular individual's path through life. With respect to the teenage years, it is the case that the experience of this life stage is fundamentally altered by the environment in which it occurs.

To understand human development, historical time is of great significance. Imagine how different life would be for a teenager growing up during World War II, or during the Great Depression of the 1930s. When we look back at the pandemic of 2020/2021, we will undoubtedly see that this global event has had a profound impact on teenagers and young adults who have lived at this time.

It is important to note that it is not just historical time that is significant here. Actual place plays its part too. Whether you grow up in an urban or rural environment will have an impact in various ways. A good example here is the fact that the availability of public transport in rural areas affects life chances. Research has shown that where public transport is scarce, and where young people live far from sexual health services, there are higher rates of teenage pregnancy. Other studies indicate that parents behave differently towards their teenagers depending on whether they live in safe or unsafe environments. Standards of housing affect health outcomes, so that the poorer the housing, the more likelihood of health risks such as obesity or other long-term conditions. There are many such examples. The point here is that both place and time are key determinants of human development.

Continuity

The concept of **continuity** underlines the fact that human development can only be understood if we look at each stage in relation to previous stages. Each stage contributes to the next one. What happens in childhood will influence what happens in the teenage years. This is especially important since so many changes follow puberty. As a result, parents sometimes experience the teenager as a "new" person arriving in the family. A chatty, cuddly and loving child may turn into a surly, uncommunicative person who pushes the parent away. How does this happen?

The notion of continuity underlines the fact that just because the teenager is showing "new" behaviour, this does not mean that there is a "new" person in the family. The young person does not arrive at the age of 12 or 13 without a history. As some people like to say, the teenager does not land from Mars as a traveller from space representing an unknown form of life! If we are able to understand the history, and what happened in childhood, we will be better able to understand the young person as a teenager.

Timing

Lifespan developmental theory emphasises the importance of the **timing** of life events. The notion of timing has to do with how life events either come all together or are spaced out. The more events come together, the harder it is to cope. This is especially significant for teenagers since a number of life events can occur at the same time. The occurrence of puberty combined with a move to a new school is a good example of this. Of course, many young people manage this perfectly well. However, if an additional life event occurs, something like a bereavement, or family breakdown, this may become more problematic.

There have been many studies on the impact of life events on the stress levels of individuals. Broadly speaking, the more life events that impact on an individual, the more stress is experienced. Where teenagers are concerned, this is highly significant. Firstly, because this is a period of major alteration in brain development, and secondly, because the very nature of the transition means that change is inevitable. These two factors mean that the timing of events is especially important. Where life events occur together there is more possibility of stress. Where life events are spaced out, things are likely to be easier for a teenager during this stage of life.

Mutuality

This refers to the point that each person in a family has an influence on others in that family. We can say that each individual reciprocally influences everyone else in the same system. This principle refers to the fact that neither parent nor teenager is an isolated entity. Each is growing and changing, and in so doing is influencing the other. The fact that the teenager is maturing will, in turn, produce changes in the parent's behaviour. However, alterations in the parents' behaviour will also have an impact on the teenager.

There are many interesting studies showing this effect. One such area of research has to do with monitoring and supervision. It may be assumed that this behaviour by the parent is determined by the beliefs the parent has about appropriate or safe behaviour for a teenager. However, studies that have looked at the long-term development of relationships show that monitoring and supervision in the parent are determined as much by the personality of the teenager as by the beliefs of the parent. The more communicative the teenager, the more likely the parent is to monitor and supervise. Even more striking is the fact that monitoring and supervision are also affected by the closeness or otherwise of the relationships during childhood, well before the boy or girl became a teenager.

Agency

I will start this section with a quote from a classic book about adolescence. "Too often adolescents are portrayed as passive recipients of circumstances ... In reality they play an active role in shaping the context in which they operate". This was written many years ago

(Feldman and Elliott, 1990), yet remains absolutely pertinent today. What do we mean by the word agency in this context?

Agency refers to the individual's ability to influence their own development. As the quote illustrates, many adults assume that teenagers are primarily affected by family, school and neighbourhood. Thus, the idea that the individual teenager is an "active agent" in shaping or determining his or her development is often seen as a novel idea. Yet a moment's thought will show how this works.

Imagine a morning in the home of a typical teenager. Even before she or he leaves the house to go to school a number of decisions have to be taken. How to manage and prepare for the day ahead? What to say to parents who are asking what is happening after school? How to respond to a series of texts that have come in since waking up? And so on. This has sometimes been described as the young person navigating a way through the everyday decisions that have to be taken. In terms of the teenage years generally, it could be described as navigating through the transitions from education to work, from home to college or independent living, from intimacy with family to intimacy with a new partner.

All this is done through having a sense of agency, an ability to shape one's own life and make one's own decisions. Clearly, there are limits to agency. Some of these are structural, to do with the way power and influence operate in the family or community. Some limits are to do with the life experiences of the individual. Time and place may be limiting factors. In the case of the coronavirus pandemic, the fact that an individual teenager was due to leave school this summer could have a significant impact on the range of options available. Other limits may be to do with life experiences such as loss or trauma.

Research into what is known as information management provides another good example of the way agency operates. This topic has to do with the way an individual manages the flow of information towards other people. Let us assume that a 15-year-old teenager has done badly on a piece of schoolwork. She gets feedback from the teacher, but what then? Does she tell her parents or keep it to herself? This decision involves information management. She will make the decision. She will navigate through this particular situation and will learn to manage the consequences. Studies in information management have shown that teenagers have complex and sophisticated processes for making these decisions. They will consider many factors when deciding what to tell and what to hold back.

To conclude, these five elements of lifespan developmental theory (time and place, continuity, timing, mutuality and agency) help us to view the teenage years in a more detailed and rounded manner. The theory enables us to take into account psychological and social factors that will affect the life course of an individual. The theory contributes to a richer perspective on the teenage years. It can be placed alongside our knowledge of brain development to give us a broader view of this stage of life.

Puberty

I want to turn now the importance of puberty. When most people talk of puberty, they think of a girl starting her periods or a boy whose voice has just broken. These are only some of the signs of a major process of change within the body that takes place any time between the ages of 9 and 14. Puberty involves a lot more than the outward signs of sexual maturation. Puberty involves changes in all organs of the body, including the lungs, the heart and other organs, including – of course – the brain. The composition of the blood alters at this time, as does the hormone balance, a topic I will return to in the next section. Here are some basic facts about puberty:

- The beginning of puberty is triggered primarily by the release of sex hormones – testosterone in the case of boys and oestrogen in the case of girls
- All the different changes associated with puberty will last about two years
- Puberty starts between one year and 18 months earlier for girls than it does for boys
- There is wide individual variation in the age of puberty and the sequence of changes. This is perfectly normal
- The average age for a girl to start her periods in Britain today is 11 years 10 months; this age dropped between 1900 and 1960 but has remained unchanged since then
- In spite of the average age being 11 years 10 months, one in five girls will have started their periods while still in primary school
- Although the age of some aspects of puberty has not changed for decades, it would appear that the start of puberty (e.g. breast bud development for girls and the voice breaking for boys) is getting

earlier. No generally agreed explanation for this has as yet been put forward
- Although the physical changes will be the obvious ones that can be seen by the outside world, there are emotional changes that can have a significant impact too.

I should emphasise that there are wide individual differences in the age at which young people experience puberty. Some can start as early as 9 or 10, while others will commence at 13 or even 14. All this is perfectly normal and has no implications for later sexual or other development. However, few of us want to stand out as being different.

Being in step, and not standing out from the crowd matters hugely to young people, and for some, this can be a painful process. Many young people get worried about the pace of change. Some worry that nothing is happening, while others worry whether the changes that are happening to them are normal or not.

There are a few individuals who start puberty either very early or very late. This can cause great anxiety for the young people who are affected and, of course, for the adults who care for them. Parents and carers need to know that none of these experiences should have lasting effects. What is critical is that adults know about the possible risks and are able to provide the necessary information and support for adolescents who experience puberty outside the expected age range.

Research has shown that boys who mature very early usually do well, as they are stronger, taller and more developed than their peers. This often means they are good at sport, something that is associated with popularity. One the other hand, boys who mature very much later than others are not necessarily popular and do not do so well in their schoolwork.

As far as girls are concerned, both early and late development can be problematic. Early puberty may lead girls into early sexual activity, often with older boys or young men. Parents and practitioners should be aware of the pubertal status of any girl or young woman who is of importance to them. Very early puberty can be an important risk factor, and girls who experience this may need additional support at this time. Very late pubertal development in young women has much the same impact as it does in boys, often leading to poor social relationships and lower school attainment.

Puberty can be very straightforward for some, and complicated for others. For some, it is a time of anxiety and stress, while others pass through it without a second thought. One key feature is that it leads to emotional changes as well as physical maturation. Puberty can have an impact on a young person's self-image and their sense of self-worth. We know from research that the self-concept of girls suffers around puberty, with nearly half of all girls feeling dissatisfied with their bodies. Puberty is closely tied up with early sexual feelings and behaviour. For those who feel vulnerable at this time, sexuality can become a very complicated aspect of life. This may lead to inappropriate relationships or risky behaviour.

One of the things that has fascinated me is the possible link between brain development and the physical changes that occur as part of puberty. Do the two things occur in tandem? Does early puberty mean advanced brain development? Or, alternatively, does a late developer struggle because brain development is also delayed? These questions seem to me to be of great interest and significance. Yet, to this point, we have very little research that sheds light on this question. I would expect that this topic will be the focus of many studies in the coming years.

Parenting

In Chapter 11 of this book, I will be discussing the development of a workshop for parents designed to give them an introduction to teenage brain development. As part of my work with parents, I have written about a framework outlining the key elements of effective parenting for teenagers (Coleman, 2018). This framework came about in response to questions I was being asked about what makes for good parenting at this stage of life.

I believe that research evidence points the way to some solid conclusions in answer to these questions. I wanted a framework that was simple and relatively easy to remember. My thinking led me to develop the STAGE framework. There are two good reasons for naming the framework in this way. In the first place, I believe it is very important to recognise that the teenage years are a stage in human development. As has been made clear in this chapter, as well as in Chapter 1, this stage has unique characteristics. The brain changes in many different ways, while the individual young person also goes through a major physical and social transition.

It is critical that adults recognise this is a stage. It is a process of change, and the behaviours of a teenager will not last forever. All too often adults believe that the unpredictable and rejecting teenager will be with them for the foreseeable future. Of course, this is not the case. This period of life represents a process, a move from childhood to maturity and change and readjustment will continue as the young person progresses towards adulthood.

The second reason for calling the framework STAGE is that each of the letters in the word represents a key element of the relationship between adult and young person. I will start with the first letter of STAGE, the letter S. This letter stands for **significance** – the significance of adults. When a teenager is refusing to cooperate, staying silent or being rude and disrespectful, it is hard to imagine that the adult has an important role to play. However, we know that adults are just as important during the teenage years as they are during childhood. They are just important in a different way.

Adults often feel they have very little influence, as the young person appears to reject what they have to say and prefers listening to friends and the peer group. Yet this is misleading. Without a relationship with a caring and trusted adult, it is so much harder for a young person to manage the challenges of this period. Parents and carers play a key role in so many aspects of life. They are role models, and their influence is absolutely critical. It may appear that their voice goes unheard, but this is an illusion. All research indicates that parents of teenagers are the key factor in future outcomes for young people.

The second letter is T – standing for **two-way communication**. Young people often say that communication with adults involves either being asked things or being told things. This is one-way communication. It is a message that goes from the adult to the young person. Yet we know that good communication involves a two-way process. All young people want to feel that they are being listened to and that their voice is heard.

Good communication between an adult and the young person involves as much listening as talking. In my book *Why won't my teenager talk to me?* (Routledge, 2018) I outline some of the reasons why communication between the generations can feel like an uphill battle. Parents and carers just need to keep in mind that teenagers really do want to talk, so long as it is a two-way rather than a one-way process.

The third letter is A – standing for **authority**. This raises the question of how adults exercise authority during the teenage years. The point here is to emphasise that the authority of an adult during adolescence cannot be based on the same principles as the use of authority during childhood. Adult authority at this stage cannot be based on power, force or punishment. The adult has a responsibility to keep the young person safe, but authority at this stage has to be based on respect and good communication. Rules will be more acceptable if they are negotiated rather than imposed. A structure has to be in place, but it has to be reasonable and take into account the age and circumstances of the young person.

The fourth letter is G – standing for the **generation gap**. Adults are sometimes too quick to judge adolescent behaviour. Such judgements can all too easily be based on the experiences of the previous generation, rather than on the experiences of today's generation of young people. Growing up today is so very different and is ever-changing. In the previous discussion on social change I made the point that factors such as social media, and the changing circumstances in education and the job market, completely alter the experience of growing up. Adults must be careful not to make judgements based on their own experiences.

The last letter in STAGE is E – standing for **emotion**. It is important to keep in mind that the management of emotion can be very difficult during the teenage years. As I noted in Chapter 1, the hormone balance is unsettled, and the brain itself takes time to mature and allow for good emotion regulation. Of course, teenagers have the capacity to arouse strong emotions in the adults around them. Adults will certainly experience anger and frustration, but their feelings may include elements of sadness, distress and even shame when things go wrong. It is essential for parents and carers to learn to recognise and manage their own emotions. It is only in this way that adults can help young people develop a better means of managing their feelings.

These then are the five elements of the STAGE framework. I set them out here as I believe they will help all readers obtain a clearer idea of what teenagers need from those around them. If the young person is to develop into a healthy adult certain features of the environment will make a real difference. Warmth and nurturance, clear structures and boundaries, not being judged on criteria of the past and help with emotion regulation will all contribute to an enriching environment. These are also the characteristics of parenting that are uniquely appropriate to the needs of the teenager during this stage of development (more detail of the STAGE framework can be found in my book *Why won't my teenager talk to me?*).

Vulnerability

I want to conclude this chapter with some thoughts about vulnerability. I will have more to say on this topic in Chapter 8 when I discuss stress and mental health. Here, I will link the concept of vulnerability with some of the ideas outlined in this chapter. In particular, I want to explore the importance of transitions in the context of lifespan developmental theory. Transitions can be especially challenging when other factors come into play. Thus, for example, where a young person has experienced disruption in relationships or personal difficulties during childhood, transitions during the teenage years will likely be additionally problematic. There are a number of reasons for this. These may include the lack of a stable attachment base, low self-esteem, inconsistency in school experiences or poor peer relationships.

Much of what has been said already can be seen to contribute to a better understanding of vulnerability. In the first place, life span developmental theory throws a spotlight on aspects of the life course that may cause increased distress or dysfunction. A good example here concerns the timing of life events. As noted earlier, when the individual experiences a range of events and stresses that all occur at the same time, it is much harder to adjust than if such events are spaced out over time.

Agency is another element of the theory that has relevance to vulnerability. As I have mentioned, most young people are able to develop agency during their teenage years so that they can gradually become more independent and self-governing. However, some factors may inhibit or restrict the development of agency. These may cause the young person to lose control over events or to engage in unsafe or self-harming behaviours. Many adverse childhood experiences, such as family breakdown or other types of trauma, would fall into this category. I should add that delayed transitions, or very rapid transitions, might leave the individual being vulnerable to experiences that severely test the resources available.

Another factor to be considered is chronological age. Although the teenage transition takes place over a number of years, it would appear that some periods during the transition are more vulnerable than others. There is good evidence to show that problem behaviours do not occur equally across the age span. A glance at the statistics concerning offending behaviour, self-harm or eating disorders shows that these troubling episodes are more likely to occur at specific ages. For example, eating disorders and self-harm among girls peak around the age of 15, while offending behaviour in males peaks at 18. This finding highlights the fact that vulnerability is influenced by the developmental process, with some problem behaviours being more likely to occur at particular ages.

As far as brain development is concerned, there are many ways in which brain activity can contribute to increased vulnerability. These may include extreme fluctuations in hormone levels, slower than normal development of the prefrontal cortex or a more difficult period of readjustment due to pruning and other changes in the major sites of the brain. It is important to recognise that the brain and the environment interact, each influencing the other. Thus, adverse aspects of the environment can impact on the way the brain develops, while at the same time, problems in brain development will influence behaviour and thus impact on the context in which the young person is growing up. This will be discussed in greater detail later in the book.

In the next chapter, I want to turn to the background of this book. I am not a neuroscientist, and for most of my career I have not concentrated on the impact of the brain on teenage development. I will now describe how it came about that I have written this book about the teacher and the teenage brain.

Further reading

Coleman, J (2011) *"The nature of adolescence: 4th edition"*. Routledge, Abingdon, Oxon.
Coleman, J (2018) *"Why won't my teenager talk to me? 2nd edition"*. Routledge, Abingdon, Oxon.
Steinberg, L (2015) *"The age of opportunity: Lessons from the new science of adolescence"*. Mariner Books, New York.
Temple-Smith, M, Moore, S and Rosenthal, D (2016) *"Sexuality in adolescence: The digital generation"*. Routledge, Abingdon, Oxon.

References

Feldman, S and Elliott, G (Eds.) (1990) *Capturing the adolescent experience* In *"At the threshold: The developing adolescent"*. Harvard University Press. Cambridge, Massachusetts. Chapter 1, page 11.

Chapter 3

From "My Baby's Brain" to "My Teen Brain"

Introduction

In this chapter, I will explain how I came to be writing a book about the teenage brain. My background is in clinical psychology, not neuroscience. I have not worked in a brain imaging laboratory. I have not carried out research on the brain. You may well ask, then: "What brought me to the point of writing this book?"

It all started with a phone call. It was at a time – in 2012 – when I was working in Oxford, at the Oxford University Department of Education. I had given a talk about adolescent development, my specialist subject. In the audience there was someone called David Silverman, who at that time was Director of Children's Services in Hertfordshire. David called me and asked if I would be willing to meet, as he needed some advice from someone who knew about teenagers!

This is the story he told me. In 2008 or thereabouts, Hertfordshire Children's Services had developed a programme entitled "My Baby's Brain". The idea behind the programme was to help all the Hertfordshire staff working in early years to be more aware of the importance of brain development. The intention was to train all staff including health visitors, social workers, nursery nurses and children's centre staff to understand something about the baby's brain. This would enable them to recognise how important it is to nurture early brain development. It would enable them to help mothers in the early stages of parenthood to recognise this too.

David had planned to roll this out for professional staff, and then follow up with films and other materials for parents and families. This programme had proved a great success, and in 2012, David and his colleague Joella Scott were looking for the next phase of this work. David and Joella had been reading in the press about new research that was appearing to do with the teenage brain. What better direction to follow than to pursue the idea of a programme on the teen brain?

"My Baby's Brain"

Before I say more about the teen brain programme, I want to outline in a bit more detail the background to "My Baby's Brain" (Figure 3.1). In order to emphasise the importance of this, the programme set out some basic information about the infant brain. This information was

Figure 3.1 Cover illustration from "My Baby's Brain" programme.

intended to show the significance of brain development and to garner interest among professionals and parents. Some examples included the fact that the brain doubles in size in the first year of life. By the first birthday the brain is two-thirds the size of an adult brain. If babies grew in height like this, they would be four feet tall at one year of age!

An introductory and advanced training was offered for professional staff. The introductory programme was entitled "Five to thrive", while the more advanced training was called "Vulnerability, trauma and recovery". The theory underlying the programme had been published and discussed in various books and journals in the preceding years.

One good example is Sue Gerhardt's book: *Why love matters* (Routledge, 2010). In this, she charts the development of the brain in the first years of life, emphasizing the powerful impact of strong attachments on healthy brain development. She also underlines the impact of poor or inadequate parenting on brain development. One of her chapters is called "Corrosive cortisol" where she discusses infant anxiety and its effects on the brain. Another section of the book is called "Shaky foundations and their consequences".

Other authors were writing similar things, but it was books like *Why love matters* that prompted David Silverman, Joella Scott and colleagues to develop "My Baby's Brain". Of course, this work was developed in the context of attachment theory, and much of the programme for professional staff drew upon this. The material in the training programme included the importance of touch and physical contact, parental gaze and attunement, the impact of stress on brain development, communication between mother and baby and other similar topics.

The programme for parents was called "Five to thrive: The things you can do every day to help your child's growing brain" (Figure 3.2). The five things were identified as:

- Talk
- Play
- Relax
- Cuddle
- Respond.

As the programme says:

These are your child's daily "five to thrive" – the building blocks for a healthy brain. A healthy brain will help your child be happy

The brain is amazing...

In the first year of life the brain doubles in size. By the first birthday the brain is two thirds the size of an adult brain. If babies grew in height like this, they could be four feet tall when they were one year old!

The brain is not like any other part of the body. Nearly all the cells of the brain are in place when we are born – about a hundred billion of them. But they are not yet working. The brain grows when connections are made between the cells in response to what is happening to us. These connections are forming all the time all through our lives. What happens to us shapes our brains.

In the first three years of life the brain is growing and changing faster than it ever will again. At times during the first year of life a million connections are forming every single second in your baby's brain.

So what happens to your baby shapes their brain. And the most important thing that happens to your baby is you! Everything you do when you are with your baby sparks connections in their brain, turning connections into pathways that the child can use again.

five to thrive

Your child's body grows better when you give the child good food. Your child's brain grows better when you do five simple things that feed the growing brain:

Respond • Cuddle • Relax • Play • **Talk**

These are your child's daily 'five to thrive' – the building blocks for a healthy brain. A healthy brain will help your child be happy in themselves, make friends and enjoy their family life, as well as being the best start for learning once they go to school. And every day will bring many opportunities to give your baby's brain what it needs to grow well.

Figure 3.2 Image illustrating the five key elements of "My Baby's Brain" programme.

in themselves, make friends and enjoy their family life. And every day will bring many opportunities to give your baby's brain what it needs to grow well, as well as being the best start for learning once they go to school.

There is no doubt that the programme has been a great success. It is still, at the time of writing (2020), running in Hertfordshire, and literally thousands of staff have gone through the training. In addition, almost all parents of infants and toddlers have been introduced to ideas about brain development as a result of this initiative.

"My Teen Brain" (1)

The Hertfordshire plan was to take the ideas behind "My Baby's Brain" and develop them further so that a similar programme could be run for staff working with teenagers. The staff team had already carried out some focus groups with students in local schools and the results were striking. Both young people and teachers had all indicated that they believed more information about teenage brain development would be useful for anyone working with this age group.

David and Joella asked me if I would help them develop this programme and act as a consultant to the team. I was certainly interested, yet cautious as I did not consider myself particularly knowledgeable about the brain. I did know something about adolescent development in general, but I was hardly an expert on brain development. However, the Hertfordshire team were persuasive. It was also true that I had become very interested in the results of research on the teenage brain that had been appearing in the literature since the advent of brain scanning around the year 2000.

I had been particularly struck by the fact that research findings were reported showing that the areas in the teenage brain relating to emotion and reward (the amygdala) were believed to be maturing at a faster rate than those to do with thinking and reasoning (the prefrontal cortex). This was leading researchers to conclude that they had now found the explanation for teenage risk-taking. In young people, thinking about consequences was lagging behind the wish to have fun!

My view was that this was too simplistic. First, I thought that there were probably large individual differences. After all, this research was in its early stages. Second, I have always been worried about the negative stereotype that attaches itself to young people. Was this just another example of an excuse to see teenagers in a bad light?

With some reservations, therefore, I agreed to assist the team in developing what came to be called "My Teen Brain". I could not do this on my own, and I was delighted that Family Links agreed to come on board and help with the training. Family Links is an organization, based in Oxford, dedicated to promoting emotional health in children and families. We were able to work together with Hertfordshire to take the first steps in exploring what "My Teen Brain" would look like.

McGill University

I am going to take a slight diversion here since my own career does have some relevance to the story. It is the case that during many years working with teenagers in hospitals, schools and academic settings, I was not at any time directly concerned with the brain and brain development. Indeed, as I have noted, up to the beginning of the 21st century, we believed that the brain stopped developing at the end of childhood.

When I look back at what I was writing in the 1990s, I see that the teenage brain was hardly mentioned. In the book I wrote with Leo Hendry, *The nature of adolescence: 3rd edition* (1999), the brain did not appear at all. When discussing puberty, we talked of the growth of the lungs and the heart, we mentioned the change in the composition of the blood, we discussed the growth spurt and many other aspects of puberty, but the brain was not included. That was because there was simply nothing to say about it! There was no research on the teenage brain, and no one saw it as relevant to our understanding of adolescence. How things have changed!

However, there is another element to this story. I did my undergraduate work in psychology at McGill University in Canada. It turned out that at that time (the 1960s), McGill had one of the most exciting centres for research on the brain anywhere in the world. It has to be said that when I chose to go to Canada, I had no idea of this fact. The Head of the Department of Psychology then was Don Hebb, a leading expert in the field. Indeed, although Hebb died in the 1980s, his theory of how the brain works is still current and can be found in any good neuroscience textbook. The saying: "Neurons that fire together wire together" is commonly known as Hebb's law.

As undergraduates, we were expected to take part in laboratory work. Usually this involved work with rats that had had electrodes implanted into various parts of their brains. In passing it should be noted that such experimental work would not be allowed today. Rules about experimentation on animals have tightened up considerably since the 1960s.

This laboratory research, whether we consider it acceptable or not, did have major implications for the understanding of brain function.

There are many examples to choose from, but here is one. Hebb and his colleagues were able to show that there was a particular area in the brain that, if stimulated, appeared to create a sensation of utter pleasure. Rats were given the choice of pressing one of two levers. If the animal pressed one lever a pellet of food appeared. The other lever led to a mild stimulation in what became known as "the pleasure centre". The results were extraordinary.

Rats would go on pressing the second lever until they dropped down from exhaustion. As soon as they woke up, they would return to the lever that gave what was assumed to be unimaginable pleasure. The offer of food was totally ignored. To watch this was mesmerizing and has stayed with me since 1960.

I remember well the speculation that was rife among the students. What if this centre existed in the human brain? Would this be an alternative to the most wonderful drug that had ever been invented? Could this be a way of controlling human behaviour? Is this what Huxley's "Brave New World" would be like?

It has been fascinating to learn that Hebb and colleagues were correct. There is indeed a centre, the *nucleus accumbens*, that works exactly as these early researchers predicted. And it exists in the human brain as well as in the brains of other species.

I tell this story to illustrate the relevance of my early experiences in studying psychology at McGill University. A lot of what I learnt in my undergraduate work has been very useful in my subsequent career. Laboratory work with rats, however, had not been particularly high on this list. Until that is, I got the call from David Silverman and started working on the "My Teen Brain" project in Hertfordshire.

"My Teen Brain" (2)

As we started planning the work necessary to develop the "My Teen Brain" programme, there were a number of questions that had to be answered. The first of these related to the participants for whom this programme was to be designed. Who was going to attend? It became clear that the intention was to provide a training programme for all those who came under the umbrella of the Children's Services team in Hertfordshire. This would then include social workers, school nurses, those working in residential centres, staff in youth offending teams and school counsellors.

This is a diverse group, and we recognised that there would no doubt be a range of experience among the attendees. Nonetheless, the core object of the delivery would have to do with developing a better understanding of teenage development, as well as providing an introduction to the changes taking place in the adolescent brain.

The next question to be addressed had to with the content of the training. Staff in the Children's Services team made it clear that the topic of risk and resilience was very high on their agenda. They wished for the content to include material that addressed this, so that staff could think through how to reduce risk-taking behaviour and enhance resilience. This was a common view in welfare services and education generally at that time. There was a belief that the way to address risky behaviour among young people was to teach resilience. The Hertfordshire team also wanted some material on parenting, as they believed that this would be a concern for the practitioners attending the course.

We then considered the structure of the training. In Hertfordshire there is a strong tradition of offering one-day training packages. It was therefore decided to design the "My Teen Brain" training to fit into this model. With the help of Family Links, we created a one-day training, containing four modules:

- An introduction to the teenage brain
- An outline of the challenges of parenting at a time of rapid brain development
- Understanding risk-taking behaviour in the context of changes in the brain
- A module on resilience through a focus on healthy brain development.

We designed the day with short presentations around these four topics, together with exercises and activities to run alongside the topics. Our style of training is an interactive one, and we were keen to allow for lots of discussion. We also created opportunities for the participants to concentrate on lessons for practice at the end of the day.

Readers will note that, in addition to material on the brain, we were including a focus on risk and resilience, as well as on parenting. I want now to say a little more about these two topics and to explain how we developed these training materials.

Risk and resilience

In 2007, Ann Hagell and I had edited a book entitled *Adolescence, risk and resilience: Against the odds*. In designing the "My Teen Brain" training, I looked back at this book, only to see that the brain was not mentioned! Nowhere in the book did we or the other authors refer to brain development or the implications of the major changes that were taking place during this stage of life. There was clearly a big task for us to find ways of linking what was known about risk and resilience with emerging knowledge about teenage brain development.

We called the risk section of the training: "Risk, or why it is hard to think ahead". This made it easy to refer to the fact that the teenage brain takes a long time to mature. We were able to explore risk and protective factors, a theme that would come up again in the section on resilience. We discussed risky thinking – egocentrism, invulnerability and so on – to show how the maturation of the social brain leads to short-term deficits. Lastly, we looked at hormones such as dopamine, illustrating how the hormone balance can easily affect behaviour.

Turning now to resilience, we noted that there were many ways to define resilience. Some work on resilience applies to those who have suffered major adversity, while other approaches concentrate on a universal model – something for all young people. We looked specifically at the relation between the areas of the brain to do with sensation and reward (the amygdala) and the areas to do with thinking and problem-solving (the prefrontal cortex). As I have already noted, much has been made of the possibility that the prefrontal cortex matures more slowly than the amygdala and the limbic system. This means that young people may be more inclined to take risks than to think in a resilient manner.

There was an opportunity to explore what resilience meant in the context of brain development. It seemed clear that to be resilient the individual would need input from the prefrontal cortex. This led us to bring in ideas of healthy brain development, by which we meant encouraging and facilitating the maturing of the prefrontal cortex. One teacher who attended an early training session was so attracted to this idea that she went back to her school and designed an assembly that she called "Beefing up your prefrontal cortex". I shall have more to say about this later in the book.

Parenting

It may at first seem strange to have included a module about parenting in a one-day training about brain development. There were a number of reasons for this. First, I had been working with Family Links to develop a series of workshops for parents that we called "Talking

Teens". We were thus very conscious of the fact that parents and carers have a pressing need for a better understanding of teenage development. Second, we were aware that a number of the participants on our course would be working with parents, many of whom might be having difficult issues with their teenage sons and daughters. Indeed, this proved to be the case in over half of all attendees.

Third, we expected that many of the individuals attending the course would themselves be parents of teenagers. Inevitably, therefore, these professionals would be acutely aware of how this material might impact on their own family life. We wanted to recognise this, and to provide some means of making the material relevant to the experiences of the participants.

We designed the module so that the links between brain development and parenting could be illuminated. We focused on the role of parents in promoting healthy brain development. We considered the teenager's development of language and related communication skills. We looked at the need for boundaries and structure in the context of the major reorganization taking place in the brain. Finally, we considered the important question of emotion regulation, showing how difficult this can be for young people due both to hormone variation and the maturing of the amygdala.

Conclusion

In thinking back over the nine years or so since we started the "My Teen Brain" programme, I can only say that it has been one of the most rewarding projects of my career. When we started there was no one doing anything like it. We were definitely in uncharted territory. And so it has remained. I keep asking colleagues if they know of other similar initiatives, and the answer is always the same. There is nothing like it, as far as they know.

Part of the problem, I think, has to do with the doubts that many people seem to have about the wisdom of trying to translate science into something useful in the classroom. A good example can be found in an article by Michael Thomas and colleagues of Birkbeck College in London (Thomas et al., 2019). Here they highlight the arguments of those who remain unconvinced about the value of this work.

It is worth pointing out why the goal of the field is a challenging one. First, the way the brain learns is complex. Second, learning is only one part of education. Third, society's goals for education are not necessarily clear. And fourth, even for psychology, successful translation from science to educational practice has proved difficult.

(p. 479)

I understand the argument, but I see education in a rather different light. To my mind, the benefits of learning about the brain are much wider than a straightforward translation to educational practice. To be fair, Thomas and colleagues do go on to explore ways that current knowledge can be useful in the classroom. They mention motivation, well-being and the social brain. All these topics will be explored in detail in the course of this book. Nonetheless, this article frequently quotes authors in the academic world who have concerns about translating scientific knowledge into educational practice. This book is my answer to them.

One of the remarkable aspects of the work I have done on the "My Teen Brain" project is how much has changed since we started in 2013. New knowledge is becoming available all the time. Good examples of this are excellent publications about the importance of sleep for young people (e.g. Walker, 2018), as well as knowledge about reward processing in this age group (e.g. Galvan, 2017).

When we began this work the experience of scanning involved lying for 30 to 40 minutes on a bed that slid into a form of tunnel. There was a lot of noise and the person being scanned had to remain still for that period of time. In these years scanning has taken huge strides, and it is now possible to carry out brain imaging without the need to lie still on a bed in a tunnel for over half an hour. This represents amazing progress, as it is now possible to extend brain imaging research to many more groups of young people and to carry it out in many different contexts.

What could be more rewarding than to help people understand new science? This new science changes our understanding of the teenage years. This knowledge has the potential to alter the way relationships between adults and young people develop. The reaction of those to whom I have presented this material speaks volumes. They report a complete shift in how they see teenagers.

"Eye-opening"; "A light bulb moment"; "This has changed my view of youngsters"; "My work will benefit enormously from this information"; "I wish I had known this earlier".

I could go on. We have delivered the training to hundreds and hundreds of professionals and parents across numerous settings. I am enormously grateful to those in Hertfordshire and the team at Family Links. Together they have given me the opportunity to take part in a project that, without exaggeration, has the potential to make a real difference to education and family life.

Further reading

Coleman, J and Hendry, L (1999) *"The nature of adolescence: 3rd edition"*. Routledge. Abingdon, Oxon.
Coleman, J and Hagell, A (Eds.) (2007) *"Adolescence: Risk and resilience: Against the odds"*. John Wiley. Chichester.
Galvan, A (2017) *"The neuroscience of adolescence"*. Cambridge University Press. Cambridge.
Gerhardt, S (2010) *"Why love matters: How affection shapes a baby's brain"*. Routledge. Abingdon, Oxon.
Walker, M (2018) *"Why we sleep: The new science of sleep and dreams"*. Allen Lane/Penguin. London.

References

Thomas, M, Ansari, D and Knowland, V (2019) "Educational neuroscience: progress and prospects". *Journal of Child Psychology and Psychiatry*. Volume 60. Number 4. Page 479.

Chapter 4

Learning and memory

Introduction

In Chapter 1, I gave a brief summary of some of the key points about brain development during the teenage years. I now want to look in more depth at some of the topics that are of particular relevance to teachers and the school environment. It is appropriate that learning and memory are the subjects to be considered first.

It is important to stress that I do not see this book as a primer on brain function. I will not be devoting a lot of space to the anatomy of the brain. I will not go into detail about the technology of brain imaging (scanning), nor will I summarise the research literature at any length. However, I will need to provide some basic information about brain function so that you, the reader, can make sense of the processes of learning and memory.

As I noted in Chapter 3, one of the criticisms levelled at educational neuroscience is that it is not much use to teachers, since it is as yet far from established. Educational neuroscience has been criticised for spending too much time arguing about theory and quibbling about research design. I understand these arguments, but I believe that the knowledge we have today can make a profound difference in education (Thomas et al. 2019).

I accept that learning is an enormously complex process. I do not see our current knowledge about the brain being able to explain every aspect of learning. However, we do know some basic facts about how learning takes place. This knowledge will help teachers understand their students. It is knowledge about teenage development, rather than knowledge about complex brain structures, that can make the difference to education.

As one teacher told me:

> I deliver this material (the Teen Brain programme) to the students, but then we go on to deliver to the teachers. It is only small parts

of the programme, but little bits too, so that they understand the students. One of the things that really stuck in their heads – the pruning – they went WOW! That really impressed them. Amazing isn't it? And then again it was mind blowing to them to know there are, what is it, 100 million neurons in the brain. Just amazing! Isn't it? The teachers found that quite fascinating.

My goal is to illustrate how information about brain development can be of use in the school environment. I also believe that basic knowledge about what happens in the brain can be of enormous benefit to young people themselves. In this chapter, I will set out what I mean by this.

How learning actually takes place

In Chapter 1, I outlined some basic information about the brain. I noted that neurons are connected to each other in patterns and networks. The brain operates by sending impulses along nerve pathways. I mentioned the role of synapses, the tiny gaps between neurons. These synapses play a critical role, as they either facilitate or hinder the continuing passage of the impulse around the brain.

Information that comes into the brain is temporarily stored in short term memory – in the hippocampus and associated structures. If the information matches with existing memories, it is discarded. On the other hand, if the information is new, it is sent out to various regions in the brain to be processed and stored for future use.

The brain is designed to attend to new information. This is essentially what learning is. The more activity there is between neurons, the stronger the synapse. You may remember I mentioned Don Hebb in Chapter 3. He is still known today for a saying that is at the heart of learning. This saying is: "What fires together wires together". This refers to the fact that the more particular neurons activate together, the more likely it is that learning will take place (Figure 4.1).

The more a piece of information is repeated or relearned, the stronger the synapse becomes. Some have described this as being like a path through a meadow. The more you walk through the long grass, the clearer and more defined the path becomes.

Two words are useful here. These are "frequency" and "recency". The more frequent and the more recent our learning, the stronger the likelihood that this learning will be successful. To put it another way, if we learn something often and if we learn it within a short period of time, then the likelihood is greater that this learning will become entrenched.

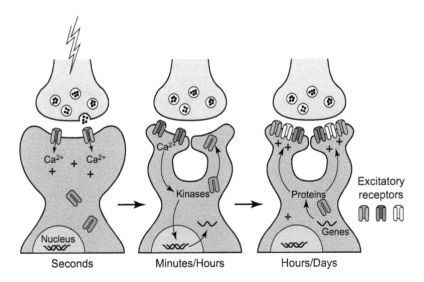

Figure 4.1 New receptors are added to synapses during learning.

The process by which learning takes place is known as long-term potentiation (LTP). If the neuronal connections are strengthened, and embedded, then it is said that long-term potentiation has occurred. In order for this to happen, both sides of the synapse have to be "on". In other words, the receptors on either side of the synapse have to be in receptive mode.

If this is the case, the synapse becomes stronger and stronger, which, in turn, causes a bigger response in the neuron that has been activated. Jensen (2015, p. 75) points out that if you are learning any of this as you read, you will be building new synapses. Only minutes after you learn something new, your synapses start to grow bigger. In a few hours, they will be cemented into a stronger form (Figure 4.2).

Figure 4.2 Illustration of the process of learning – the more you walk through a field of long grass, the more defined the path becomes.

I noted in Chapter 1 that there are both "on" and "off" receptors in the brain. What if the receptor on either side of the synapse is an "off" receptor? This is the process by which the brain manages the flow of information. As you can imagine, at any one moment the brain is flooded with new sensory input, as well as messages from various organs, muscles and glands that control hormones. The brain needs to screen out some information otherwise it would be overwhelmed. This is the function of the receptors that inhibit the flow of information around the brain.

One of the features of brain development that contributes to learning is the process of pruning. I pointed out in Chapter 1 that this is a profoundly important element of the changes in the brain that occur during the teenage years. Connections between neurons that are no longer needed are allowed to die away, while those that are of value become embedded. Some have called this process "neural Darwinism", in that the "fittest" survive. In this sense, "fittest" means those that are most used.

It is counterintuitive to learn that some parts of the brain actually reduce during this period. In this case, one could say that less means more! Or to put it another way, the brain becomes a "leaner, meaner" machine – a more efficient machine. A graph showing the decline in grey matter is illustrated in Figure 4.3.

The brain does not only consist of grey matter. While the grey matter clusters around the outside of the cortex, there is the white matter in the middle of the cortex to be taken into account. It is the white matter where most of the connections between neurons lie, and this part of the brain actually increases in size during the teenage years. So, while we have a reduction in grey matter, at the same time, other areas of the brain are growing (Figure 4.4).

Finally in this section, I want to refer to the concept of brain **plasticity**. This is a term often used to describe the capacity of the brain to repair itself. This may be following a traumatic incident, such as a traffic accident, or it may be due to illness or disease. However, plasticity also refers to the adaptability of the brain as it responds to pruning and the other changes that follow from this.

Plasticity of the brain during the teenage years allows for increased learning capacity. The connectivity between the two hemispheres develops and the brain responds to these changes, becoming a better learning machine. Adolescence is one of the stages of life when there is a truly rapid development of learning capability.

Because there is so much change happening, it is reasonable to see this stage of life as a "sensitive period" as far as the brain is concerned. This means that what happens during this phase of life really

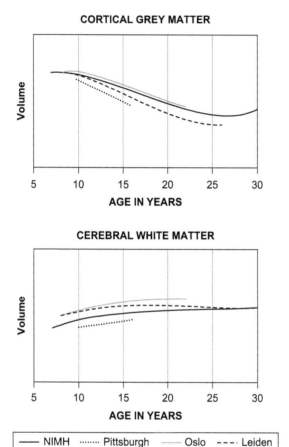

Figure 4.3 Graphs showing the development of white and grey matter from ages 5 to 30. (Mills, K et.al. (2016). Structural brain development between childhood and adulthood. *Neuroimage*, 141, 273–281.)

matters. Learning experiences during the teenage years have long-term implications for future development. It also means that, even when things have not gone well during earlier periods of schooling, there is an important window of opportunity during the teenage years. One teacher expressed this well when she said:

> One thing I found particularly powerful, knowing that the years of puberty are so significant. For the teens who have had a

disadvantaged start, you feel that they are behind and are never going to catch up. Ideas about the changing brain can be very empowering for teachers. To know that it is a significant time, it is here and now, and it is something I can do something about. We do always want teachers not to feel that – well – what's the point? The teacher is already in a difficult situation, what can we do in school? It is important to bring it out – things are changing. It is not all set, and that is what the brain stuff tells you.

What is learning, what is memory?

Most writers in neuroscience make little distinction between these two concepts. However, it seems important to explore this a little further. In the first instance, it can be argued that memory is a **capacity**, while learning is a **process**. Furthermore, memory is essentially dependent on the resources or capabilities of the brain, while learning will be influenced by a wider range of factors, such as the family, the school environment and the teacher, as well as individual factors such as motivation and interest in the subject.

In learning a poem, as an example, one could either say you were memorizing it or you could say you were learning it. In this case, the two words are interchangeable. However, you would not say someone was memorizing how to drive, but you would say they were learning how to drive. A trainee chef would not be memorizing how to cook.

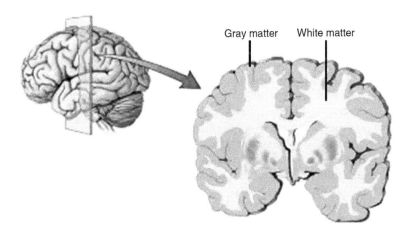

Figure 4.4 Illustration of white and grey matter in the cortex.

Such a person would be learning how to cook (of course, they might be memorizing a recipe, but that just illustrates the point). So, in the case of activities that involve a range of skills, it is more usual to refer to the process as learning. When it is a case of rote learning, we are more likely to use the word memory. But there is the conundrum. I have just used the words "learning" and "memory" in the same sentence. How can we tell them apart?

Many writers make a distinction between **declarative** and **nondeclarative** memory. The first is considered to be representational, referring to our ability to recall facts and bring events and information into consciousness. This aspect of memory is most closely associated with the hippocampus and associated brain structures. Nondeclarative memory refers to habits and routines linked to performance of one sort or another. A good example might be riding a bicycle, where we carry out an activity without much thought or effort. As far as the brain is concerned, nondeclarative memories are likely to be located in areas such as the spinal cord, the amygdala and the striatum.

In most cases, those concerned with neuroscience and education have used the two terms interchangeably. In this book, I started by trying to keep the two things distinct. In the end, however, I found this to be very difficult. Memory and learning are often indistinguishable in the English language. I have accepted this and followed most other authors in letting the meaning of the sentence determine how I have used the two words.

Executive function

Executive function is one of the key concepts used for understanding the increasing capacity of the brain during the teenage years. Executive function is the term used to describe certain processes that underlie learning. In the field of neuroscience relating to education, there has been much interest in executive function. There are good studies showing that executive function is closely related to academic performance. Thomas et al. (2020) quote research indicating that executive function skills are predictive of achievement in school. These skills are believed to predict up to a third of the variance in mathematics and reading scores.

It is generally considered that there are four elements that make up executive function. These are:

- Working memory
- Inhibition

- Resisting interference
- Flexibility.

I want now to explore these four elements, starting with **working memory**. Working memory refers to our ability to hold a certain amount of information in our attention while we are processing it. This is a key skill and can be shown to increase gradually from infancy onwards. It is significant for our understanding of learning in the teenage years, as it is a capability that can be seen to underpin intellectual activity. Here again this is a concept that was considered to have been fully developed by the end of childhood. It is only with the advent of scanning and the extraordinary increase of our understanding of brain development that we now know that working memory, among other skills, continues to develop throughout the adolescent years.

Working memory can be measured by varying the amount of time between the presentation of a stimulus and retrieving the information. Another way of assessing working memory is to vary the amount of information rather than the timing. Readers will be familiar with the parlour game of placing a number of objects on a tray, giving a certain time for those playing to memorise the objects and then asking how many can be recalled.

This can be replicated in the laboratory, where the number of objects to be memorised can be varied. In one task there may be ten objects, and this number can be increased gradually to test working memory at different ages. Crone (2017) reports studies showing that working memory, tested in this way, improves during childhood and up to the age of 15. The changes between ages 11 and 15 are smaller than those in childhood.

A different approach to studying working memory is to ask the participant to reorganise the material while they memorise it. For example, they may be presented with a random string of letters – P, V, A, R, G, N, B. In order to memorise these letters, the subject needs to find a way of linking them together, and this is a harder task. Here, the differences between teenagers and adults are more marked. The individual has to do some work in order to carry out the memory task, and this probably involves different parts of the prefrontal cortex working together. Research shows that this skill only develops gradually during the teenage years (Crone, 2017).

Working memory is an essential skill needed for many of the activities taking place in the classroom. A mathematics or science problem that requires the manipulation of figures or other types of information will be dependent on working memory. Designing schedules or planning activities during the school day, as well as subjects as varied as music and language, all utilise working memory.

Several research studies have looked at different brain regions and their activity during working memory tasks. What is clear is that regions of the brain gradually become more developed as working memory improves. Different parts of the prefrontal cortex become more mature, thus underpinning the development of working memory. Studies have shown that during childhood, brain activity is diffuse across different regions of the brain, while during the teenage years the areas related to working memory become more developed and brain activity during working memory tasks begins to look more like the adult brain.

We can now turn to the next element of executive function – that of **inhibition**. The skill implied here is the ability to stop oneself from doing something or to attend to one stimulus while ignoring another. This is an essential capacity for learning. In the brain, the ability to activate inhibition depends on the receptors that I noted earlier – what are known as the off receptors. These are the ones that prevent or inhibit the passage of a message along the nerve fibres.

There are a multitude of ways in which inhibition plays a part in learning. In fact, it would not be possible to pay attention in class without the ability to inhibit stimuli in the surrounding environment (e.g. other pupils, the view out of the window), as well as stimuli from inside the body (e.g. hunger, thirst, tiredness). In addition, inhibition is essential for learning, since new learning often involves un-learning old material. Thirdly, we make assumptions about our environment depending on what is obvious around us. A good example is the idea that the world is round. It looks flat, but we have to inhibit that idea to learn that it is, in fact, round.

Inhibition is measured in the laboratory using various tasks. The most well-known is the stop-go task. Here, the individual is asked to press a button if a certain type of picture is presented. This might be a red dog. The individual has to go on pressing the button as long as red dogs are shown, but not when the picture shows a blue dog. The task is to see how quickly the individual can adapt to the changing picture.

A more sophisticated task is the stop-signal task. The individual is faced with a task much like a traffic signal. One response is required if the signal points one way, another response if the signal points the other way. This is easy if there is time to recognise the difference, but it becomes harder when the signal alters quickly, or if there is little time to respond. Research has shown that the ability to inhibit increases with age. Different regions of the brain are activated by the inhibitory response. Slowly, over time, the teenage brain begins to look similar to the adult brain when faced with situations such as the stop-signal task.

Now we can look at the next element of executive function – that of the ability to **resist interference**. I have already noted situations where it is necessary to ignore extraneous or irrelevant stimuli. Concentrating in class would not be possible without this ability. However, sometimes the distraction is located in the task itself. In this instance, the individual has to screen out some aspects of the task in order to complete the task. Reading inhibition is a good example of this. The Stroop task illustrates this nicely.

The task was named after John Ridley Stroop, who developed the task in the 1930s. It has been used ever since to demonstrate resistance to interference. The task is very simple. The individual is shown a picture of the word red, and the letters are red. The task is to name the colour. This is easy when the colour of the letters corresponds to the word. However, when the word is GREEN, but the letters are blue, the task becomes that much more difficult (Figure 4.5).

The areas of the brain needed to perform the Stroop test keep changing and maturing all through the teenage years. The older the adolescent, the better he or she is at suppressing irrelevant information. A particular area of the frontal cortex is critical here (the lateral frontal cortex), and this area has been shown to mature well into the twenties. Thus, although those in the 12–14-year age range are good at restraining their actions, as in the stop-go task, they have much greater difficulty in suppressing interference.

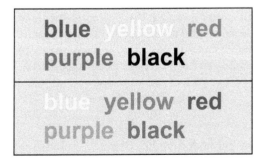

Figure 4.5 Stroop test illustrating interference. One element of the image contradicts the other.

The last of the four elements of executive function is **flexibility**. Many would argue that this skill is essential for learning and memory. Flexibility is needed when we learn new skills. Why? Because in most situations learning requires feedback about how we are getting on. Are we doing something correctly, or have we made an error? If we have made an error, then we need to correct it before we can continue with our learning.

Flexibility has been investigated using tasks where individuals are required to apply rules (e.g. to respond to the presentation of a certain colour) and are then given feedback about whether it was right or wrong. Once a participant has been responding correctly for a while, the rule can be changed abruptly. The individual has to use the feedback to work out the new rule. In this research, it is possible to test the flexibility of the participant. Here again, this skill can be shown to increase with age.

Research has shown that feedback indicating that behaviour is incorrect leads to activation in two brain areas in the frontal cortex connected to purposeful behaviour. Crone (2017) calls this system of the brain the "alarm" system because it becomes active when people make mistakes. In one study, Crone and colleagues looked at 14–15-year-olds and found that these areas of the brain had not yet become mature. A further study showed that as individuals grow older, they are more able to recruit these areas of the brain to respond when they make mistakes. The more individuals recruited these areas of the brain, the more they learned to adapt their behaviour to the demands of the task.

Research is consistent in demonstrating that the four elements of executive function mature during the teenage years. These skills can be shown to correspond to maturation in defined areas of the brain, namely the prefrontal cortex and the frontal cortex. This is significant because there seems little doubt now that the various elements of executive function underlie learning and are associated with academic performance. The more we understand of executive function, the more we can understand how the ability to learn accelerates during the teenage years.

Types of learning

It is time now to consider how our understanding of executive function contributes to useful knowledge about young people. I will start with **working memory**. It will be self-evident that working memory has its limits, and this then restricts how much information the individual has at their disposal at any one time. This is demonstrated in our everyday life when we make shopping lists or put a telephone number in our smartphone. We cannot hold more than a certain amount of information in our minds at one moment, and we therefore need to find ways of helping our memory out.

In terms of classroom activity, we can assist students to think about this in order to lift the load on working memory. Many young people will face difficulties when faced with new learning. One way of dealing with this is to encourage students to articulate the processes they are using to solve problems. This may be through writing things down or by documenting the steps taken to arrive at a solution.

This has been demonstrated in research on brain activity during problem-solving activities. When students are first introduced to a problem, let us say a mathematics problem, they tend to use a range of locations in the frontal cortex. With practice brain activity alters. As students become more familiar with strategies to reduce the load on working memory, shifts can be detected in brain activity. When learning processes become more automatic, brain activity is reduced and relocated to different sites in the cortex (for a summary of this work, see Howard-Jones, 2010).

Another question that is of importance to students is how best to learn new material. A useful finding arising out of research on brain activity has to do with the different modes of learning. For many years, scientific evidence has demonstrated that learning in more than one mode at a time can enhance memory. This evidence has underpinned the design of what is known as **multi-modal approaches** to education.

It is now possible, however, to show the links between such approaches and activity in the brain. Thus, we now know that visual and verbal learning is associated with arousal in different regions of the brain. Where both regions of the brain are engaged in learning tasks, there is a clear advantage for students. An additive effect occurs so that when more than one brain region is engaged in a learning task, that learning is likely to be more successful (Crone, 2017).

This leads on to a discussion of **visualization**. Studies show that the process of visualizing an object uses nearly as many locations in the brain as happens when we actually see the same object in front of us. As a result, it will be evident that the use of mental imagery will prove a powerful tool in any learning activity. The importance of visualization is related to another idea, that of **vicarious learning**.

There has been much discussion in the literature of what are known as mirror neurons (Gazzola et al., 2007). These are neurons that fire when we observe the behaviour of other people. The interesting thing here is that mirror neurons react in much the same way as they would do if we were behaving in a similar way ourselves. This effect can even be seen if we simply hear a report of someone's behaviour. These findings are important in that they emphasise the power of visualization. They also point to the potential of visualization in classroom activities.

I will now turn to another topic: the impact on students of **learning about the brain**. Since the premise of this book is that knowledge of brain development can be of value both to teachers and students, this research evidence is of great interest. Howard-Jones (2010) reports a series of studies in which it was demonstrated that learning about the brain was beneficial for other types of learning.

In the first study, students were told one of two things. One group was told that intelligence was malleable and could change over time as young people matured. The second group was told that intelligence was a fixed entity. Interestingly, the first group showed significant improvement in their academic performance in subsequent years.

In the same study, the authors (Blackwell et al., 2007) reported another study with low-achieving students. Here, the pupils were told about brain structure, how learning changes the brain by producing new neurons and new connections. They also gave a clear message that students themselves had some agency over the process. In other words, it was up to them. The results were striking. Grades for the group that had received this information improved markedly, while those who had not received this input continued on a downward trajectory.

To my knowledge, there have been no other studies like this. Nonetheless, the results are striking, and of great importance. They provide support for the basic "My Teen Brain" premise. They demonstrate that by providing students with simple facts about brain development it is possible to make a difference to learning outcomes. It will be obvious that, for teachers, it will be of great value to have some idea of how the brain works in the learning process. It is also the case that this information can make a major difference to students themselves. I explore this in greater detail in Chapter 10 when I discuss the lesson plan I have developed to help young people learn more about how their brains work.

Conclusion

Learning and memory are topics of profound importance to teachers. In this chapter, I have shown how our knowledge has gradually increased in recent years. I argue that, in spite of reservations in the world of academic educational neuroscience, this knowledge is central both for those who impart information in the classroom and those who receive it, namely the students themselves. I have outlined the concept of executive function and illustrated the way the four elements of executive function – working memory, inhibition, resistance to interference and flexibility – all contribute to learning. Research on the brain throws light on these aspects of cognitive function. I have explored types of learning such as multi-modal learning and vicarious learning. Finally, I have demonstrated that information about brain development can have a direct impact on student performance in the classroom. More research on this subject is badly needed. For the present, it will be apparent that this important finding provides corroboration for the approach taken in this book, as outlined in Chapters 9, 10 and 11.

Further reading

Blakemore, S-J (2019) *"Inventing ourselves: the secret life of the teenage brain"*. Transworld Publishers/Penguin, London.

Crone, E (2017) *"The adolescent brain: Changes in learning, decision-making and social relations"*. Psychology Press/Routledge, Abingdon, Oxon.

Howard-Jones, P (2010) *"Introducing neuro-educational research: Neuroscience, education and the brain"*. Routledge, Abingdon, Oxon.

Jensen, F (2015) *"The teenage brain: A neuroscientist's survival guide to raising adolescents and young adults"*. Harper, New York.

Thomas, M, Mareschal, D and Dumontheil, I (Eds.) (2020) *"Educational neuroscience: Development across the life span"*. Routledge, Abingdon, Oxon.

References

Blackwell, L et al. (2007) "Implicit theories of intelligence predict achievement across adolescent transitions". *Child Development*. Volume 78. Pages 246–263.

Gazzola, V et al. (2007) "The mirror neuron system". *NeuroImage*. Volume 35.

Thomas, M, Ansari, D and Knowland, V (2019) "Educational neuroscience: Progress and prospects". *Journal of Child Psychology and Psychiatry*. Volume 60. Number 4. Page 479.

Chapter 5

Risk and reward

Introduction

Risk is a common topic in discussions about teenagers. Why do they behave in the way they do? In previous chapters, I have already mentioned the idea of teenagers as risk-takers. There has been evidence from brain research that has provided corroboration of this notion due to the way the brain develops during these years. In this chapter, I will explore the science behind these notions. I will also outline recent thinking to do with the special place that rewards play for this age group and indicate why I believe this evidence has particular relevance for teachers.

Risk

Larry Steinberg outlines a theory of adolescent risk-taking in his book *The age of opportunity* (Mariner Books, 2015). The argument is that the brain's limbic system, which includes the amygdala, matures earlier than the prefrontal cortex. Thus, the part of the brain that seeks the positive feelings associated with having fun and taking risks is, at times, more powerful than the area designed to manage behaviour and inhibit risk-taking.

The discrepancy in maturation between the two areas of the brain has been called a "developmental mismatch". Although all parts of the brain are maturing, the areas associated with risk are out of step with the areas associated with reasoning and problem-solving. As a result, teenagers are not always able to stop themselves doing things in the heat of the moment, even if such behaviour may not be entirely sensible. This theory has also been referred to as the "dual systems model", because of the two brain systems involved.

There have been numerous attempts to investigate this theory. Sarah-Jayne Blakemore (2019) provides good evidence to support the notion of a "developmental mismatch". With colleagues, she looked at thousands of brain scans and carried out an analysis of the average development in three regions of the brain. The three regions she studied were the amygdala (which processes emotion), the nucleus accumbens (which processes reward) (see Figure 5.1) and the prefrontal cortex.

She reported that, indeed, there are differences in the rates of maturation between these regions. The grey matter in the amygdala increases slowly up to the age of 14 but does not change after that. The grey matter in the nucleus accumbens slowly declines during the teenage years. In contrast, the grey matter in the prefrontal cortex declines sharply during these years, losing 17% of its volume. Thus, it will be apparent that development in the three regions differs markedly (Figure 5.2).

This is not the whole story. As Blakemore points out, these findings relate to the **average** for a whole population. When you come to look at individuals, the picture looks rather different. As can be seen from Figure 5.3, there are very large individual differences in the way these three brain regions develop from ages 10 to 30. This is an extremely

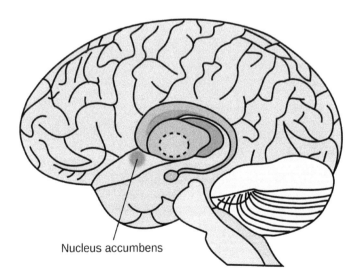

Nucleus accumbens

Figure 5.1 Simplified image of the brain showing the position of the nucleus accumbens.

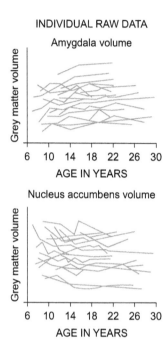

INDIVIDUAL RAW DATA

Amygdala volume

Nucleus accumbens volume

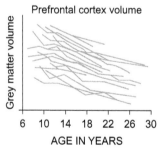

Prefrontal cortex volume

Figure 5.2 Individual raw data for changes in grey matter volume in three sites of the brain. (Tamnes, C et.al. (2017). Development of the cerebral cortex across adolescence. *Journal of Neuroscience*, 37, 3402–3412.)

important finding and shows just how important it is to recognise that we are not all the same.

This evidence from brain imaging shows that developmental mismatch is more marked in some individuals than in others.

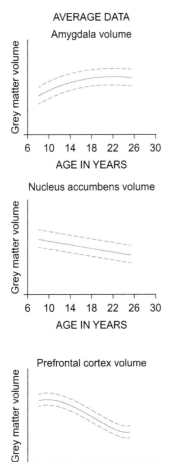

AVERAGE DATA

Amygdala volume

Nucleus accumbens volume

Prefrontal cortex volume

Figure 5.3 Average changes in grey matter volume in three sites of the brain. (Tamnes, C et al. (2017). Development of the cerebral cortex across adolescence. *Journal of Neuroscience*, 37, 3402–3412.)

Furthermore, there are some young people whose brains show no indication of this feature at all. Translating these findings into our understanding of risk-taking, we can see that the links between this behaviour and brain development are far from clear. Not all teenagers will take risks. Those who might take a risk will not do so every time an opportunity arises. Even among those who do risky things, not all will be harmful.

The "trainee adult"

It could be argued that the idea of a poorly functioning or immature brain gives a one-sided view of teenage development. Dan Romer (2003), of the Annenberg Public Policy Center in the United States, has made a powerful case for an alternative view of brain development in young people. As he writes: "Brain deficits don't make teens do risky things: lack of experience and a drive to explore the world are the real factors" (p. 32).

Romer, and other writers who take a similar view, believe that there is a good reason why the teenage brain works as it does. These authors argue that risk-taking reflects a biological drive for exploration. This process is fundamental in allowing young people to seek novelty and acquire experience. This is a stage in the life course when learning about oneself and the world around one is vital for the transition to adulthood. Without this experimentation, it would not be possible to grow and mature.

In the work that I do, I sometimes use the phrase "trainee adult" when explaining this process. I point out that we do not expect trainees to get things right first time around. We expect, and allow for, some mistakes in the learning process. In the same way, young people are learning how to grow up. As part of this process, they are bound to make mistakes along the way. They may choose unsuitable friends, they may stay out late when that is not a wise thing to do and, of course, they may drink too much at a party. Which of us has not done so?

"Hot" and "cold" risk-taking

There have been many laboratory studies trying to understand how the teenage brain works in the context of risk-taking. One classic study (the Iowa Gambling Task) uses different packs of cards. Participants are asked to choose between different packs. The options involve using one pack that offers small but frequent rewards or to use another pack where large rewards are offered that occur only rarely. This pack also contains cards that lead to large losses. A pack such as this is classified as the "risky" pack. Such a situation mimics a typical gambling experience. High reward with high risk or low reward with less risk.

Results show that adults and young people behave differently in such scenarios. The likelihood that participants will choose the risky pack is highest in the adolescent group. Some in this age group continue to use the risky pack, even though they lose money as a result. On the contrary, adults are more likely to select the low-risk cards. When they do start with the risky pack, they soon move over to the lower risk cards when they see they are losing money.

One important caveat should be noted here. Researchers have made a distinction between "hot" and "cold" situations. Where money is involved, this could be described as a "hot" situation. Brain imaging shows that areas of the brain associated with reward processing are more active in such situations. However, when the situation could be described as a "cold" situation, where there is no emotional content, teenagers and adults behave in ways that are much more similar.

If a young person is on their own, with time to think about a risky choice, she or he is no more likely to take that risk than an adult. On the other hand, if this teenager is at a party, surrounded by friends, in a "hot" situation, she or he might be more likely to make a risky decision.

It is essential to stress here that there are substantial individual differences in risk-taking. Indeed, some young people avoid any risky behaviour. Others might be tempted to take a risk on rare occasions, perhaps only once or twice, but would for the rest of the time stay clear of risky choices. Alternatively, there are some, perhaps those who are more impulsive, who will be risk-takers. As the work of Sarah-Jayne Blakemore has shown, it is apparent from brain scans that individuals differ hugely in the way they develop through the teenage years.

Dopamine

I have been talking so far as if the way the brain develops is the only factor influencing risk-taking in young people. It is time now to mention other factors. The first of these is the hormone dopamine. This hormone is known as the reward hormone. I included a short section on the role of hormones in Chapter 1. It is now time to return to this topic. We know that there are literally dozens of hormones that are active in our brains at any one moment. One of the most important as far as teenagers are concerned is dopamine.

Dopamine plays a big role in the teenage brain. There are more dopamine receptors in the young person's brain than there are in the adult brain. Dopamine has two functions. On the one hand, it encourages behaviour that may lead to a reward or the sensation of pleasure. It also has a separate role, in that dopamine is released following a reward, causing a feeling of well-being and satisfaction.

In her book on the teenage brain, Adriana Galvan (2017) discusses the role of dopamine. She notes that many studies, using both animal and human brains, have shown a peak level of release of dopamine during the adolescent period. As she says: "Together these data suggest that, during adolescence, changes in dopamine neuro-chemistry may alter reward sensitivity in response to drugs, social interactions and consummatory behavior" (p. 155).

In other words, the fact that more dopamine is likely to be released in the teenage brain means that during this stage individuals are more sensitive to the potential rewards that come from using drugs, going to parties or eating fast food and sugary snacks.

We should keep in mind that there are individual differences in the level of dopamine in any one brain. Nonetheless, it is important to recognise that, in some situations, it may be that dopamine levels play a part in stimulating or encouraging behaviour that involves risk and reward. Readers may be interested to learn that a practice known as "dopamine fasting" has become popular among adults in the United States and the UK. In essence, this means practising calm, meditative behaviour. Awareness of dopamine and its effect on behaviour is reaching a wider public. This knowledge should extend to an awareness of the role of dopamine in the teenage brain.

The peer group

Another important factor with the potential to influence risky behaviour is the peer group. Before I begin this discussion, I wish to underline the fact that a peer group can and does play a positive role during the teenage years. There are many ways in which friends and the wider peer group contribute in a beneficial way to the lives of young people. They offer a setting for the learning of social skills. They offer support at a time in life when it may be hard to seek that support in the family. They offer companionship. They offer a context in which to discover the adult world and to explore questions of identity. All this is true, and there are many other examples of the positive role played by the peer group.

Having said this, I will now turn to an alternative perspective. There have been many studies illustrating the way in which the peer group influences teenage risk-taking behaviour. The classic investigation is the one concerning risky behaviour behind the wheel of a car. This is known as the Stoplight Task, reported first by Larry Steinberg and colleagues in 2005. Here the task is to drive in a simulator around a racetrack. The object of the task is to get around the track in the fastest time possible. During the task, various hazards are presented such as a red light appearing or a pedestrian wandering into the road.

There are two conditions. In the first condition, teenagers, young adults and older adults are all on their own when they drive around the track. In the second condition, the participants are asked to bring a couple of friends to watch them drive around the track. The results are striking. In the first condition, there are no differences between the age groups in the number of risks they take. In the second task, however, the level of risk-taking is significantly higher in the adolescent group of drivers.

These results illustrate the fact that, when in a social situation, young people are more likely to take risks than they would if they were on their own. These data are supported by information from insurance companies. If a comparison is made between traffic accidents in the under-25 age group and accidents involving older drivers, then the same result becomes apparent. Accidents involving under-25s usually occur when there are other people in the car. On the other hand, accidents among older drivers are more likely to occur when the driver is alone in the car.

To conclude, many factors contribute to risky behaviour. While the "developmental mismatch" theory may provide part of the picture, there are obviously other elements to consider. We also have to keep in mind that there are wide individual differences. No two teenagers will react in the same way in a situation where there is an option to take a risk. I am also attracted to the idea that, in some senses, risk-taking is an important feature of teenage development. If we shift our perspective, some behaviours can be seen as experimentation rather than risk-taking. The brain may be constructed so that during these years the young person is encouraged to explore and seek new experiences. We need to be very careful before we fall into the trap of accepting the "broken brain" model to describe this age group.

Reward processing

It could be said that reward processing is simply the reverse of the coin we call risk. Why do people take risks? In many cases, it is because they are attracted by the rewards associated with that behaviour. Examples might include having fun at a party, the buzz associated with going on a fairground ride or eating too much chocolate. In fact, I have already referred to reward when discussing dopamine. I noted that dopamine is known as the reward hormone and that its release in the brain leads to the seeking of pleasure and enjoyment.

The question of whether the teenage brain processes reward in the same way as the adult brain has been one of the key concerns of researchers in this field. I will outline one or two studies that have looked at this topic. The findings are of great interest. I should note that this has direct relevance to the classroom. Educators are concerned with motivation. What motivates students to work hard, to concentrate in class, to do well in exams? An understanding of reward processing may contribute to this debate.

It might be worth mentioning here a point I made in Chapter 3 when I was talking about my own undergraduate experiences at McGill University. Readers will remember that I told the story of the experiments carried out in the university by Don Hebb and his colleagues, J. Olds and B. Milner (1954). Here it was shown that if rats could obtain stimulation to a certain part of the brain, they would go on doing this until they were exhausted. This site in the brain came to be known as the reward centre. We now know that the nucleus accumbens is the site in the brain identified by Hebb and colleagues all those years ago.

It is time to consider studies of reward processing in humans. One of the earliest studies in the modern era employed a "Wheel of Fortune" task (Ernst et al., 2005). In this task, the participants are asked to spin the wheel and the number it lands on determines whether you win a reward or not. Both adults and young people take part while their brains are being scanned. The results showed that young people demonstrate more activity in the reward processing area of the brain (the nucleus accumbens) than adults when they win on the task. The task is then made more complex by varying the amount of money that can be won. Regardless of whether the reward is large or small, teenage brains are more active than those of adults.

Another study illustrating this phenomenon is that carried out by Galvan and colleagues (2006). In this study, the participants are shown three cues on a computer screen, each cue associated with a different level of reward. The goal is to identify the cue that gives the greatest reward. The earnings associated with each cue are then shown on the screen so that participants get feedback on how much reward they will receive.

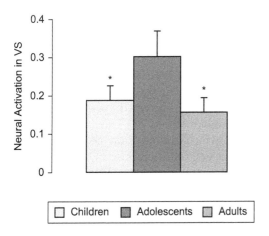

Figure 5.4 Degree of activation in the ventral striatum in three age groups when offered a monetary reward. (Illustrated in Galvan, A (2017) *The Neuroscience of Adolescence.* Cambridge University Press. Cambridge.)

The results indicate that the areas in the brain associated with reward are activated to a greater degree in adolescents than in other groups. Furthermore, these areas continue to show a higher level of activation for a longer period after the reward in the teenage participants. This difference is illustrated in Figure 5.4.

Galvan and McGlennen (2013) also report an interesting study that compares different types of reward. In this study, the investigators offered both a monetary reward and one that consisted of a sugary drink. The results showed that young people are more responsive to the rewards of both sugary water and money than the adult participants. In addition, the teenage participants found the sugary water more pleasurable than the adults, and this difference was apparent in brain activation. We can conclude from these and other studies that the nucleus accumbens and other parts of the limbic system are hypersensitive to reward during the teenage years.

Conclusion

In the course of this chapter, I have covered a number of themes that have relevance for teachers. First, it is essential to remember just how much adjustment and restructuring is taking place in the teenage brain. When young people appear confused or uncertain, it is worth considering how much change is going on in their brains. Second, I have noted the area in the brain, including the amygdala, which is attuned to reward at this time. Rewards assume greater significance for this age group than they do for other age groups.

Next, and related to this, the role of the hormone dopamine has to be taken into account. There is more dopamine in the teenage brain than there is in the adult brain. Levels of hormones such as dopamine also vary to a greater degree than in other age groups. As well as dopamine I noted the importance of the peer group. In some situations, especially those that might be described as "hot" situations, young people may be more influenced by the presence of the peer group than they would be in more relaxed or neutral situations.

I mentioned the concept of the "trainee adult". This refers to the fact that young people are learning and experimenting in all sorts of ways at this stage in their lives. Teenagers will make mistakes. Behaviour that can, at first sight, appear senseless or idiotic may occur as a result of inexperience. This is particularly important in schools, as learning does not just apply to maths or geography. Other types of learning are taking place, especially to do with behaviour in social situations.

Finally, it is worth underlining the significance of reward for teenagers. When adults are looking for factors that will influence behaviour, rewards should come top of the list. This is often overlooked. Teenagers tend to receive more criticism than praise from the adults around them. Research on the brain clearly shows that teenagers will be more motivated by reward than by any other feedback. This single fact can make a significant difference in the way teachers and pupils interact. Schools would do well to take into account these results from brain research.

Further reading

Blakemore, S-J (2019) *"Inventing ourselves: The secret life of the teenage brain"*. Transworld Publishers/Penguin, London.

Galvan, A (2017) *"The neuroscience of adolescence"*. Cambridge University Press, Cambridge.

Steinberg, L (2015) *"The age of opportunity: Lessons from the new science of adolescence"*. Mariner Books, New York.

References

Ernst, M et al. (2005) "Amygdala and nucleus accumbens in responses to receipt and omission of gains in adults and adolescents". *NeuroImage*. Volume 25. Pages 1279–1291.

Galvan, A et al. (2006) "Earlier development of the nucleus accumbens relative to the orbitofrontal cortex might underlie risk-taking". *Journal of Neuroscience*. Volume 26. Pages 6885–6892.

Galvan, A and McGlennen, K (2013) "Enhanced striatal sensitivity to aversive reinforcement in adolescents versus adults". *Cognitive Neuroscience*. Volume 25. Pages 284–296.

Olds, J and Milner, P (1954) "Positive reinforcement produced by electrical stimulation of septal area and other regions of rat brain". *Journal of Comparative Physiology and Psychology*. Volume 47. Pages 419–427.

Romer, D (2003) *"Reducing adolescent risk: Towards an integrated strategy"*. Sage Press. New York. Page 32.

Chapter 6

The social brain

Introduction

In the first chapter, I briefly outlined what is meant by the social brain. This is the area of the brain that understands other people and develops skills necessary for social interaction. I noted that, as part of the changes in the brain, new skills become available to the teenager. These skills are essential as the social world becomes wider and more complex. However, the growth of these new skills is far from straightforward. In some areas there appears to be a pause, or even a dip, in the capacity to understand others. The young person may become preoccupied with the self, a phase that is sometimes labelled "adolescent egocentrism".

In this chapter, I will first outline some of the cognitive processes that underpin the development of social skills. I will then go on to explore the main social skills that mature during this stage. I will look at the recognition of emotion and perspective-taking. Finally, I will discuss social evaluation and outline some of the interesting findings on what has come to be called "social pain".

Cognitive development

Many writers have noted that social skills depend on the cognitive maturation that is taking place during these years. Social skills and new ways of thinking go hand in hand. What are these new ways of thinking? Firstly, teenagers develop the capacity to think about future possibilities. They are not limited by a focus on the present. Young people become able to switch between the concrete situation (the here and now) and abstract possibilities (the future).

Thinking in abstract terms allows other changes to take place. The individual can see that many situations are not clear-cut – either good or bad, right or left. Individuals begin to recognise the grey areas and see that the world is more complex than it was perceived to be in childhood. Abstract thinking also allows for scientific reasoning. Implicit in any science is the ability to test out hypotheses. If I do this, what will follow? How does one process or experiment differ from another? How can I compare the two?

There are some other important aspects of cognitive maturation. One of these is what has been called metacognition. This refers to the ability to evaluate one's own thoughts. Did I get that right? Should I have approached it differently? How could I have changed my thinking? It is this skill that underlies the ability to think about other people's thoughts too. Lastly, there is the skill to look at things from different angles. This is sometimes considered as being able to consider the multiple dimensions of a problem.

As we will see, all these elements of cognitive development play a part in the growth of social skills. Here is the question. Do these skills develop independently of teaching and learning in school, or are they a result of school experiences? This is something that has been endlessly debated. Readers will not be surprised to learn that teaching and brain development interact together. It is neither one nor the other, but both. As I have noted earlier, the brain and the environment work together to produce a mature individual.

We have known since the very early days of research on the brain that rich environments lead to healthy brain development, while impoverished environments restrict brain development. To show this, we can return to our friend, Don Hebb. In the 1950s, Hebb proposed what he called the **Environmental Complexity Paradigm**. In the laboratory, he created three different environments in which animals matured. The first cage was full of interesting objects to create a stimulating environment, the second was a somewhat more boring cage and the third had very little in it.

When Hebb and his colleagues looked at the brain development of these animals, they found that the more stimulating the environment the healthier the brain. The animals that had grown up in the most stimulating environment were better at solving problems and quicker at learning new tasks.

Can we translate these findings into the human sphere? In terms of restricted environments, the closest example would be growing up in poverty. There have been many studies on poverty and its impact on brain development. These are well summarised in Galvan (2017). In brief, the results show that the more restricted the environment, the greater the effect on the development of a healthy brain. There are many possible explanations for this finding, including the impact of poor housing, less access to good quality health care and, of course, less stimulation in the early years.

There is an important caveat here. The teenage years can be described as a "sensitive period" as far as brain development is concerned. This is a time of huge change, and thus, also a time of great opportunity. Experiences that are positive and enriching during these years can make a significant difference. Even when earlier experiences have been far from ideal, there is a window of opportunity following puberty. It is at this time that the brain undergoes major change. If this change can be coupled with support and stimulation at school, much can be achieved to overcome earlier experiences.

Having looked at the development of cognitive skills, we can now consider how these underpin social skills. The changes that take place during these years include the following: the recognition of emotion, perspective-taking and social evaluation. Each of these skills has been the subject of considerable research. This is not surprising. As the social world of the teenager widens the skills that allow safe navigation of the social space become more important. This was always the case when relationships primarily occurred in the physical world. Today, however, with many relationships and interactions taking place online and through social media, these skills become even more significant.

Emotion recognition

Recognition of emotion in the human face may at first appear to be a very basic skill. However, it is an essential aspect of the ability to stay safe in social situations, manage conflict and respond appropriately when with other people. Knowing when someone is angry from the expression on their face is a good example of such a skill. To be able to do this successfully often determines the outcome of an interaction.

Research has highlighted three key findings concerning the recognition of emotion. The first is that there is a specific area in the brain dedicated to facial recognition. This is known as the **fusiform face area**. This is in the temporal lobe of the cortex, located at the back of the brain with close links to areas to do with vision. We know that this area plays a vital role in facial recognition, since when it is damaged the individual has great difficulty in recognizing faces. The fusiform face area also has links to other areas which play a role in the interpretation of faces. All of these can be shown to mature as the young person gets older and cognitive skills improve.

The second finding is that the recognition of emotion becomes progressively more sophisticated. While some emotions such as happiness or sadness can be recognised by children as young as three or four, the recognition of more complex emotions only becomes possible during the teenage years. Emotions which show in the face such as surprise and fear are harder to interpret. The ability to recognise these emotions only develops gradually as individuals move into adolescence.

The third finding is that, in young people, the amygdala plays a key role in emotion recognition. A number of studies have shown that in teenagers the amygdala is much more engaged in facial recognition than it is in adults. As a result, the teenager is more likely to be influenced by his or her own emotions when recognizing emotion in others. This of course may lead to confusion or an error in recognition. Some writers have called the amygdala the "agent of change in adolescent neural networks" (Galvan, 2017). This means that the amygdala is playing a greater role in the development of social skills, allowing emotion to be more influential in teenagers than in adults.

Perspective-taking

Perspective-taking is an important social skill. We cannot form or maintain social relationships without being able to see situations from another person's point of view. Crone (2017) makes the point that perspective-taking is an essential skill for the development of autonomy. Autonomy involves the ability to think for oneself and behave independently. This requires awareness of different beliefs and attitudes, and the ability to choose between them.

Scientists have referred to this ability as mentalizing. In other words, when we mentalise we think about the thoughts of other people. Work on this topic is also sometimes described as having a *theory of mind*. To have such a theory implies that we have a theory of how other people are thinking.

A description of the process whereby we think about other people's thoughts has been suggested by Nelson and colleagues (2016) as the **social information processing model**. This involves three areas of the brain. The first is the area related to vision, concerning the detection of stimuli such as the appearance of the face, gestures and other nonverbal cues. The second area has to do with the processing of emotion, while the third area concerns both memory and reasoning. This last area is the one we have described as the prefrontal cortex, although some other areas of the frontal cortex are also involved.

These areas of the brain have to work together. How does this develop? Sometime between the ages of three and five children begin to understand that other people think or see things differently from their own way of thinking. However, this form of perspective-taking is limited. It might involve understanding that someone is sad when they are happy, or that the room looks different if you look at it from the other end. What is known as social perspective-taking takes longer to develop.

Social perspective-taking involves not only being able to ascribe complex emotions to other people, it also involves being able to see things from a third person's perspective. A good example would be the realization that the behaviour of one friend may impact the feelings of another friend, even when one's own feelings are different from those of both friends.

It has always been assumed that perspective-taking gradually improves with age, improving markedly during the teenage years. Some studies show that the more complex elements of perspective-taking continue to improve into early adulthood. Researchers have used a variety of methods to study this phenomenon. One common form of research involves participants being told stories about other people so that comparisons can be made between neutral situations and ones where emotions are engaged.

An example might be one story that involves a friend who becomes nasty to you even though you have just helped her with her schoolwork, and another where you and a friend are getting on a bus to go home and chatting about the school day. Researchers can then look at which areas of the brain are activated in these two different situations.

Another good example of research looking at this social skill is described by Blakemore (2019) as the Director Task. Here the participant is asked to move objects on open and closed shelves from the viewpoint of themselves or of the Director. The Director is standing on the other side of the cabinet, and thus has a different viewpoint of the open and closed shelves. This situation is illustrated in Figure 6.1.

The task for the participant is to move only those objects that can be seen by the Director on the other side of the screen. The ability to carry out this task does indeed improve with age. What is of particular interest is that the skill continues to improve up until early adulthood. This illustrates the fact that the areas in the brain needed for this task take a long time to reach full maturity.

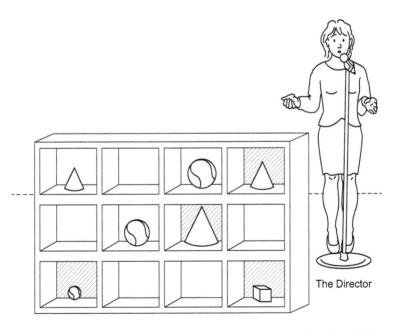

The Director

Figure 6.1 The director task. Image illustrating perspective-taking from different positions. Based on a similar image from Blakemore, S-J (2018) *Inventing Ourselves: The Secret Life of the Teenage Brain.* Transworld Publishers/ Penguin, London.

This finding was further elaborated through the design of a modified version of the Director Task. In this second version, there was no actual Director, simply some shelves with a dark background and some with a light background. In this second task, the participants had to follow the instruction "Never move objects that have a dark grey background". This, therefore, can be described as non-social perspective-taking. What is intriguing is that on this second task both teenagers and adults showed the same developmental pattern. It is only on social perspective-taking where teenagers take longer to reach the same level as adults.

Social evaluation

The term "social evaluation" is the term taken to refer to the way young people judge or evaluate themselves as they interact with others in social situations. This is linked with the concept of adolescent egocentrism. The individual starts to become aware of how he or she looks to others, and this leads to a time of social sensitivity.

Let us consider what is happening here. Two aspects of development come together. In the first place, puberty leads to a changing body. There is an alteration in the way young people look to themselves, and, therefore, to the world around them. Not surprisingly, young people become sensitive about their appearance. Research shows that nearly half of all teenage girls feel dissatisfied with their bodies. The figure is lower for boys, but there is still a significant group who worry about how they look.

Combined with a changing appearance, there is the ability to think about what others think. This is the mentalizing skill that I have described previously. The young person starts to consider how other people view them. As the body changes, and as identity questions start to come to the fore, the young person can become "pre-occupied with the self". A nice way to think about this is to reflect on what has been called "the imaginary audience". The teenager spends time imaging that they are on stage. The whole world is looking, and this can lead to intense self-consciousness.

This self-consciousness very often leads to a stage when the young person becomes so focused on their own world that it becomes impossible to think about others. This is what has come to be called "adolescent egocentrism". One father described this to me as follows: "When they get to this stage they go into a long, long tunnel and all they can see at the end of the tunnel is themselves".

All of us who know teenagers will recognise this feature of growing up. We can now consider how research has tackled this topic. Self-consciousness has been demonstrated through studies that create situations where teenagers are being observed by others. In one such study, young people were told that, while they were in the scanner, they were being observed through a video link by other teenagers. These teenagers reported more embarrassment, and greater activation of areas in the brain to do with anxiety than adult participants.

Another similar study placed young people and adults behind a one-way screen. On the other side of the screen was a corridor where people were constantly walking by. The participants knew that the onlookers could see them, but they could not see the onlookers. An area of the brain close to the area related to physical pain was activated in such a situation. For this reason, embarrassment has been called "social pain". Interestingly, the adults quickly adjusted to the situation, and activation in their brains calmed down. For teenagers, however, this activation reached higher levels and continued for much longer.

We know that acceptance by the peer group plays a big part in the lives of young people. For this reason, social evaluations come to assume a high level of significance. The fear of rejection can be crippling in this age group. It is not surprising that observation by others has a greater impact on brain functions for teenagers than it does for adults.

It is important to recognise that these new social skills are not the ones that are usually the focus of attention in the school curriculum.

However, they are underpinned by a wide range of cognitive skills – these are the ones on which teachers usually concentrate. Social and cognitive skills develop hand in hand. There are wide individual differences in the speed and the manner in which these skills come to the fore.

The deployment of such skills can be witnessed in the popularity and status of individuals within peer groups. There is no doubt that the more popular individuals will be the ones who have the most advanced social skills. We still know little about how such skills develop. It is probable that this development is partly related to the growth of cognitive skills but is also to do with role models and social learning in the family setting.

Readers should note that being socially skilled is relevant not only within the peer group outside school. These skills also make a difference in the classroom. Such skills will have an impact on the way student and teacher relate to each other. The level of social skills within the classroom will also have a big impact on the way work is carried out, and the degree to which collaboration between students is possible. Social skills are not just important for the playground. It should also be noted that having poor social skills may lead to rejection and isolation within the group.

Conclusion

To conclude, I will give an example of how such skills operate. While a teenage girl is in a group of peers, she thinks she hears someone make a nasty remark about her best friend. What does she do? She has to assess the emotion on the face of the person who made the remark, but also the emotions of others in the group. She then has to decide on a course of action. She weighs up different alternatives, using her memory of other social situations, evaluating the impact of the various options, and working out what the others are thinking. A situation like this involves a huge range of brain functions, all of which have to take place within a few seconds.

Learning how to manage social relationships, how to form friendship bonds and how to keep oneself safe within a group are hugely important features of growing up. As I have shown, these skills, as well as many others, are directly linked to the maturation of the brain. All these skills offer positive advantages in relationships with other key figures, both adults and peers. In addition, I have also shown how brain development leads to some short-term deficits. Preoccupation with the self and the notion of the imaginary audience refers to some of the limitations that occur during this particular stage. It is useful if teachers are aware of both the benefits and limitations of the development of social skills during the teenage years.

Further reading

Blakemore, S-J (2019) *"Inventing ourselves: The secret life of the teenage brain"*. Transworld Publishers/Penguin, London.

Crone, E (2017) *"The adolescent brain: Changes in learning, decision-making and social relations"*. Psychology Press/Routledge, Abingdon, Oxon.

Galvan, A (2017) *"The neuroscience of adolescence"*. Cambridge University Press, Cambridge.

References

Nelson, E, Jarcho, J and Guyer, A (2016) "Social re-orientation and brain development: An expanded updated review". *Developmental Cognitive Neuroscience*. Volume 17. Pages 118–127.

Chapter 7

Teenagers and sleep

Introduction

Most readers will be aware that the sleep patterns of teenagers differ in important ways from those of adults. This finding has been one of the significant outcomes of the last decades of research on brain development in this age group. As part of my work with students, I developed what I call the Change Questionnaire. I wanted to find out what students thought about the changes that had taken place for them since they became a teenager. The Questionnaire is described in more detail in Chapter 10 and Appendix 1. One of the topics in the Questionnaire has to do with sleep and based on the answers to this question I can see that approximately three out of every four students say they have difficulty getting to sleep. This means that the majority of teenagers are struggling with their sleep. This figure underlines the importance of the topic for health and well-being.

It is worth noting that 25% of this age group do not experience these difficulties. Some teenagers appear to go through this stage without any issues to do with sleep. Furthermore, there is wide variation in the timing of the change in sleep pattern. Some find this change happens to them shortly after puberty, while others manage quite well until they reach college age. Individual differences are important here as with so many other aspects of development in the teenage years.

Our lives are structured so that young people have to fit into the adult daily timetable. The timing of the start of the adult working day means that the sleep needs of teenagers take second place. There have been some attempts to address this problem, and I will have more to say about this later in the chapter. However, the priority in our daily routines is to fit with the working lives of adults. It has proved hard to make any shift in this pattern.

Research shows that teenagers need more sleep than adults. Placed in a sleep laboratory, young people are likely to sleep for between nine and ten hours. However, in the real world, teenagers are getting significantly less sleep. Surveys differ, but it is clear that many young people are only getting six or seven hours of sleep during the week (see Sharman et al., 2020). For a variety of reasons, sleep is especially important for this age group, and so the lack of sleep has very important implications.

In this chapter, I will review what happens during sleep, and I will show why sleep matters for young people. I will consider the link between sleep and learning, and then review the impact of sleep deprivation. I will discuss some of the interventions that have been developed to address the sleep problem, and I will conclude by considering why the teenage sleep pattern has developed differently from that of adults.

The teenage sleep pattern

Our sleep pattern is governed by what is known as the circadian rhythm. This is essentially a 24- hour body clock that is biologically determined (Figure 7.1). A good example of this is the fluctuation in our body temperature. This goes up and down, dipping at night and returning to a slightly higher level during the day. This rhythm continues no matter what we are doing during the day or night.

As far as sleep is concerned, melatonin is the hormone that indicates that it is time for bed. This hormone is released in the brain, sending the signal that we need to sleep. Again, it is the circadian rhythm that governs the release of melatonin. For most adults, this hormone is released in the brain at approximately the same time every evening – say, at 10.30 or 11.00. We have now learnt that the circadian rhythm works in a slightly different manner for most teenagers. For this group, the release of melatonin is delayed, usually by about an hour and a half to two hours later than in adults. The teenage circadian rhythm has shifted forwards, meaning that at the time that adults are ready for bed, the teenager's body clock is still in the phase of wakefulness (Figure 7.2).

This fact has profound implications for the life of a teenager. On weekends or during holidays, young people can sleep on in the morning, getting much-needed sleep. However, during school days this

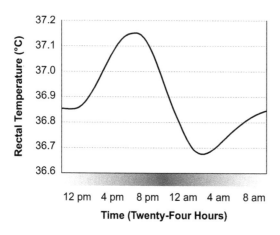

Figure 7.1 Body temperature over 24 hours showing typical circadian rhythm.

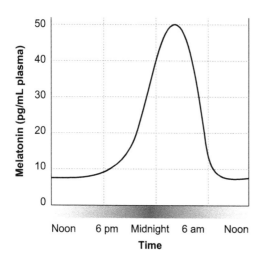

Figure 7.2 The 24-hour cycle of melatonin illustrating high levels at night time.

is not possible. As a result, it is common for teenagers to miss out on sufficient sleep during weekdays. Because of the body clock, and because melatonin is released later at night, it means that there is still some melatonin active in the teenage brain on waking in the morning. The result of this is that teenagers may well remain drowsy during the first hour or so in class. It is interesting to note that adults have virtually no melatonin left in the brain when they wake in the mornings.

There are other factors that need to be taken into account that affect sleep patterns. One of the most important of these is artificial light. Numerous experiments have shown that the presence of electric light can delay the release of melatonin. Thus, a teenager reading in a bedroom with bright lights switched on is likely to experience an even later release of melatonin. In addition, electric light from lamps or from ceiling lights is not the only source of light. We now know that the LED light in smartphones or laptops also influences the release of melatonin. The more a young person is exposed to artificial light, the more they are likely to experience a delay in melatonin release and therefore a delay in becoming sleepy at night.

Many commentators have argued that the reason young people find it hard to get to sleep has more to do with social media than with melatonin. If teenagers are absorbed by what is happening online, or if they need to be alert to texts and other digital activities, then it is not surprising that they may find it hard to switch off at night. This phenomenon has been named FOMO (fear of missing out).

There is no doubt that the pressures and enticements of the online world are very powerful. Adults have discovered this too! Nonetheless, the melatonin effect is very real. Studies have shown that, even when the young person has no digital devices in the bedroom, the body clock still works in the same way. Melatonin release is still delayed, and, as a result, it takes longer for the teenager to become sleepy (see Jensen, 2015).

What actually happens during sleep?

It is now time to turn to an examination of what actually happens during sleep. For the purposes of simplicity, I will distinguish between two phases of sleep. One is known as deep sleep when there are no rapid eye movements (NREM sleep). The other phase is REM sleep, when rapid eye movements take place, when sleep is shallower and when it is likely that dreaming is occurring. There is normally a greater proportion of deep sleep (NREM) early in the sleep cycle, and as the night continues more REM sleep occurs. As I have made clear, sleep is not only a necessity for us all, but it also has special importance for the teenage population. Why should this be so?

First, it is during sleep that essential growth hormones are released. It will not be necessary for me to spell out the significance of this. The teenage years are a time of maturation and development in all parts of the body. This is of prime importance during puberty, but the body continues to grow and develop all through the teenage years. As a result, the more opportunity there is for growth hormones to be released, the more likely it is that the physical development of the body will be facilitated.

The second finding from recent research is that certain phases of sleep are linked to the process of pruning that I discussed in Chapter 1. Pruning is the process whereby the unwanted neurons and connections are allowed to die away, making room for more efficient brain function. Studies have shown that the intensity of deep sleep (NREM sleep) increases in line with an increase in pruning during the teenage years. Then, as the brain gradually matures, and the pruning dies down, the proportion of deep sleep during the night also decreases. From this, we can see that the essential movement towards maturation in the brain is closely linked to patterns of sleep during this stage of life.

There is one further process that I wish to highlight that occurs during sleep. The brain is, of course, hugely active during the day. One of the results of this activity is the production of waste material surrounding the neurons. The waste comes from both chemical and electrical processes associated with the firing of neurons. As the neurons fire, sending signals around the brain, they create waste products. One necessity for a fully functioning brain is to have these waste products cleared up after a day's activity. This is the role of some types of glial cells. Some have called these cells helper cells, as they provide support for the brain in various ways. One particular type of glial cell acts a little like a vacuum cleaner, clearing away the rubbish and cleaning up the neurons on which our brain depends. I must be careful not to over-simplify this particular story. There are many different glial cells, so this applies to just one of this type of cell. Also, it is important to note that glial cells do not do this work on their own. They work with other structures and systems within the brain to take on the maintenance role. These processes do not only occur during sleep, but the majority of this activity is in the evening. I should note that this is a relatively recent field of investigation, and we are discovering new information as research into the role of glial cells continues. Nonetheless, the lesson is clear – without sufficient sleep, glial cells cannot do their job. We need our brains to be cleaned up every night, otherwise, we will not function well the next day.

Sleep and learning

I will now turn to some of the associations between sleep and learning. It has long been known that sleep can enhance memory. Indeed, Greek philosophers even wrote about this. However, it was not until the 1950s, when REM and NREM sleep were better understood, that we learnt more about the process of memory consolidation. Studies compared those who had more or less of the two phases of sleep, and the results were clear. It is during deep sleep that memory consolidation takes place.

Recent research has given us more information about how memory consolidation actually works. By putting electrodes on different parts of the brain during sleep, it is possible to identify the processes taking place at night. In essence, the slow brainwaves of deep sleep operate as a postal service, sending packets of information from the short-term memory store located in the hippocampus to the long-term store in the cortex at the front of the brain. It is truly remarkable that we are now able to understand this process. It appears that even a short nap during the day can lead to memory consolidation, so long as there is sufficient deep sleep during this time.

Another way of looking at this is to explore how the timing of learning impacts on memory. Many experiments have shown that the later in the day an individual is engaged in learning new material, the better the retention will be on the following day. Here is one good example. One group of learners were asked to memorise a task early in the day. After each training session, the participants showed improvement in their recall. This is known as the practice effect.

However, when tested the next morning, there was a slight loss of the material. They had forgotten some aspects of the task. A second group did the same task, but this task was carried out before they went to bed at night. The results were remarkable. When these participants returned the next night, they did not show any evidence of forgetting. Indeed, they were able to start additional learning straight away.

It is clear that going to sleep immediately after a learning task enhances memory. The reason has to do with the amount of interference taking place during the day. If one learns in the morning then the amount of information the brain absorbs during the whole day is enormous. This material interferes with the learning process. If one learns at night, the interference is much less, enabling the brain to absorb new material more easily.

Sleep deprivation

As I said at the beginning of this chapter, if teenagers are becoming sleepy later at night, and having to get up for school early in the morning, they will be missing out on the sleep they need. There has been a high degree of interest in how this reduction in sleep affects the individual. The term "sleep deprivation" is used to describe this situation. However, there is clearly a very wide variation in the amount of sleep loss experienced by different individuals. It is important to be clear about how much sleep loss is being considered.

Most commentators agree that less than seven hours sleep a night for a teenager would be considered to reflect genuine sleep deprivation. Numerous studies have reported that such an experience, especially if it continues over time, is likely to lead to a variety of emotional and behavioural difficulties. One good example has to do with the impact of sleep deprivation on learning. Two groups of teenagers are asked to memorise a task during the day. One group is able to sleep normally the next night, while the other group has their sleep continually interrupted. This second group experiences sleep deprivation, and the differences are clear. Those who are getting less sleep show poorer memory the next day.

Many studies have attempted to investigate sleep deprivation and its impact on school performance. There are two ways to do this. Loss of sleep can be artificially created by arranging for groups of students to have less sleep and then comparing their learning in school. The second way to explore this question is to consider schools that have varied their start times in the morning. There are no available data on this in the UK, but there are a number of studies that have considered this issue in the United States.

Looking at the first method, it should be said that the results vary from study to study. Broadly speaking, however, the findings show that the greater sleep loss the student experiences, the poorer their academic performance. In one large Swedish study, it was shown that the students who experienced sleep loss were more likely to fail on at least one subject in exams (see Titova et al., 2015).

Where school start times can be compared, again the results illustrate that the later the start of the school day, the better the academic performance. One study compared different high schools in Minnesota. In this case, one group of schools started the day at 7.30, while another group started at 8.40. The students in the second group of schools had better grades and demonstrated fewer episodes of depression (Bowers and Moyer, 2017).

This leads on to the question of sleep deprivation and student well-being. There are many studies that illustrate the fact that high levels of sleep deprivation have an impact on mental health. The most common finding is that sleep deprivation affects mood, and leads to higher levels of depression, as noted in the study in Minnesota. However, loss of sleep has been shown to be linked to other aspects of mental health, such as substance misuse and conduct disorders. Some studies have compared sleep deprivation of fewer than seven hours a night with sleep deprivation of fewer than five hours a night. It is evident from such studies that the greater the loss of sleep, the greater the impact on mental health. Those having less than five hours of sleep a night are twice as likely to demonstrate poor learning and higher levels of mental health problems (Sharman et al., 2020).

Interventions

There are three different types of intervention that may be noted as having tried to address the problem of teenage sleep loss. The first has already been mentioned – the option of delaying school start times so that students can sleep later in the morning. The second intervention is one that introduces what are known as "sleep lessons" or "sleep hygiene lessons" in school. The object here is to inform students about the importance of sleep and encourage them to find ways of improving their sleep patterns. Lastly, there is the work with parents, as described in Chapter 11. It is discussions in a workshop of this type that can give mothers and fathers greater confidence to address the issue of teenage sleep.

As I have noted, the option of delayed start times for schools has not proved popular in the UK. There have been one or two schools that have explored this possibility, but parents and teachers have resisted the idea. This is not surprising, since altering start times has an impact on so many other aspects of adult working lives. Some sixth form colleges have found this easier to introduce since students are mostly making their way to school on their own. However, the concept of later school starts simply has not taken root in the UK.

The situation is different in the United States. Here there has been significant pressure from groups such as the American Academy of Pediatrics and the National Sleep Foundation. There has been much discussion at a national level about this topic. In addition, individual states can make their own rules about education matters, allowing for greater flexibility. As a result, many states have made significant changes to their procedures. As one example, California introduced legislation in 2019 mandating all high schools to move to later start times. In the USA, some high schools have been starting at 7.30 or 8.00 in the morning, and many states have now legislated that school should start no earlier than 8.30.

The research evidence does bear out the need to address this problem. Where start times have been moved to a later point in the morning, the evidence shows improved school performance, fewer accidents on the road (teenagers can drive at an earlier age in the USA) and a lower level of mental health problems. In one interesting example, high schools not only moved to a later start time but also arranged the curriculum so that tests and exams were not allowed before 10.00 a.m. When comparisons were made with the previous arrangements, it became clear that achievement in tests improved significantly if performance was measured later in the morning (Sharman et al., 2020).

Turning now to the question of sleep lessons, a good example comes from the "Teensleep" study carried out in ten secondary schools in the UK. This study, based in Oxford, involved four sessions with students across the age range and involved information about sleep as well as assistance in understanding what constitutes good sleep routines. The results indicated a significant increase in knowledge about sleep, but only a very moderate change in actual sleep behaviour (Sharman et al., 2020)

For readers it is worth noting that the following strategies are suggested as contributing to better sleep and a greater likelihood of overcoming the melatonin effect:

- Turning off digital devices for a period before sleep
- If possible, putting smartphones and other devices outside the bedroom
- Turning lights low
- Using mood music or other activities to aid relaxation
- Having a hot drink (a drink without caffeine)
- Most important – getting into a regular bedtime routine.

An intervention study in Australia on sleep education looked at four different conditions. These were: sleep education plus parental involvement; sleep education on its own; sleep education plus bright light therapy; and a control group that received no input at all. Interestingly, all the sleep education conditions led to students sleeping longer at night. Parental involvement did have an effect, but only to a small degree (Bonnar et al., 2015). To sum up, as there is an increasing awareness of the role that sleep plays in our well-being and our intellectual performance, I believe that this will become a topic of greater significance in the future. It is clear that finding ways to allow or encourage teenagers to get more sleep does have an impact on the way they function in the school environment. Nothing could be more important than that.

Conclusion

I will conclude this chapter with a brief consideration of the question: why should the teenage sleep pattern be different from that of adults?

I can find two different suggestions that have been put forwards to explain this fact. One is an explanation rooted in evolutionary theory. In this theory, it is proposed that many thousands of years ago, when humans were still nomadic, it was essential for a watch to be kept at night in case of predators or warring tribes. The role of keeping watch at night was given to the younger members who were just reaching adulthood. The longer they could stay awake, the better for the tribe. Thus, melatonin release gradually altered to help those keeping watch to avoid sleep for longer into the night.

A second explanation has to do with the social circumstances of adolescent development. For young people to grow into independence they need time apart from their parents. If they can stay awake later at night, then time becomes available for them to pursue their own activities, no longer being monitored by the adults in the family. Both these explanations have some merit. I will leave the reader to decide which appears most plausible. My money is on the first of these explanations, but it may be that both play their part in explaining the remarkable phenomenon of delayed melatonin release in teenagers.

Further reading

Crone, E (2017) *"The adolescent brain: Changes in learning, decision-making and social relations"*. Psychology Press/Routledge, Abingdon, Oxon. Pages 5–6.

Jensen, F (2015) *"The teenage brain: A neuroscientist's survival guide to raising adolescents and young adults"*. Harper, New York. Chapter 5.

Sharman, R, Illingworth, G and Harvey, C-J (2020) The neuroscience of sleep and its relation to educational outcomes. In *"Educational neuroscience: Developments across the lifespan"*. Thomas, M, Mareschal, D and Dumontheil, I (Eds.) Routledge, Abingdon, Oxon. Chapter 13.

Walker, M (2018) *"Why we sleep: The new science of sleep and dreams"*. Allen Lane/Penguin, London.

References

Bonnar, D et al. (2015) "Evaluation of novel school-based interventions for adolescent sleep problems". *Sleep Health*. Volume 1. Pages 66–74.

Bowers, J and Moyer, A (2017) "Effect of school start time on students' sleep duration, daytime sleepiness and attendance: a meta-analysis". *Sleep Health*. Volume 3. Pages 423–431.

Titova, O et al. (2015) "Sleep and academic performance at school". *Sleep Medicine*. Volume 16. Pages 87–93.

Chapter 8

Stress and mental health

Introduction

It appears that stress is an ever-present feature in the lives of teenagers. In my Change Questionnaire (see Appendix 1) I asked whether, since they had become a teenager, young people were experiencing more or less stress. The answer was unequivocal – 95% responded by saying that they experienced more stress at this time in their lives. This was the most clear-cut response of all in the questionnaire.

Why should this be so? When I ask adults what they think is the reason for this result, most believe that the major stressor for teenagers is social media. However, this answer does not accord with the answers given by young people themselves. The major reason given by them has to do with school. The sorts of answers I get go something like this:

- "Pressure from teachers"
- "Pressure from school"
- "Tests"
- "Revision"
- "Homework"
- "Worry about grades"
- "Exams, exams, exams".

While this is the first reason given, family comes next, including problems at home or with parents. After that comes friends, then health issues and then social media, which is a long way down the list.

I should note that these responses were collected before March 2020, and the arrival of Covid-19. It would certainly have been the case that health issues and the impact of the pandemic would have featured if I had collected this information in the summer of 2020 or in

2021. It is also the case that the experience of education has changed substantially as a result of the lockdowns of 2020 and 2021, with most students having an extended period out of school. In addition, the fact that exams have been cancelled has added to the uncertainty experienced, especially by those in Years 11 and 13. At the time of writing, we have no idea how the changes to education as a result of the pandemic will impact on the experiences of young people in the coming years.

In this chapter, I will consider the relation between stress and brain function, and, in particular, I will look at how stress affects the teenage brain. I will discuss the links between stress and learning, before turning to topics related to mental health. I will ask whether there are higher levels of mental health problems in teenagers today, and I will then review evidence on attention deficit hyperactivity disorder (ADHD) and autism. I will go on to look at childhood trauma and consider the role of social media and its impact on mental health. I will conclude with some thoughts about the impact of Covid-19 and the lockdowns of 2020 and 2021 on young people and their mental health.

How stress affects the brain

When there is a discussion of stress the phrase "fight or flight" is often mentioned. In essence, the body releases two main chemical messengers in response to the presence of a stressor. One of these is adrenaline, the other cortisol. These chemicals prepare the body for a response that will protect the individual from threat. In other words, these substances in the body enable the individual to respond to danger by raising the heart rate, increasing oxygen levels, redirecting blood to the muscles and so on. These responses are part of our primitive history when we lived in times of ever-present danger. Today, threat comes in many different forms, and the "fight or flight" response may not necessarily be appropriate.

As noted previously, stress for teenagers may come in the form of anxiety about exams, conflict with parents, rejection within the peer group and from many other social circumstances. We have learnt a considerable amount about how stress affects the teenage brain. In particular, we now know that the brains of young people do not respond in the same way to stress as adult brains.

Stress affects the amygdala and other areas of the brain to do with the processing of emotion. The teenage amygdala has less capacity to deal with fear or anger, thus leading to more extreme responses to these emotions. The emotions of worry, anxiety and other similar feelings are all associated with levels of cortisol in the brain, and research has shown that cortisol levels are somewhat higher in adolescence than in adulthood.

The second point to make is that studies of self-control throw an important light on the way young people respond to stress. Studies of this sort place individuals in situations where a good decision involves holding back until more information is available. When teenagers are calm and relaxed, they show just as much self-control as adults. They can hold back and show a capacity to assess situations in a mature fashion. However, under conditions of high emotion, the self-control of an adolescent deteriorates, leading to poor decision-making. This finding is linked to the discussion about "hot" and "cold" risk-taking in Chapter 5. Here it was pointed out that teenagers may be able to think about consequences in some situations, but where emotion is involved (in "hot" situations), then risk-taking is more likely to occur.

Looking at brain function in such circumstances, it would appear that self-control involves using more regions of the brain. The more demanding the task, the greater the individual depends on brain connectivity. In adults, this connectivity is still present, even under stressful conditions. In teenagers, however, it is clear that such connectivity deteriorates in stressful or emotional circumstances. The older the individual, the more advanced the capacity of the brain to utilise the prefrontal cortex and therefore to manage stress. To put it another way, in teenagers, the circuits between the prefrontal cortex and the amygdala are not yet fully mature.

Stress and learning

It has long been known that there is a relation between stress and learning. Indeed, in my undergraduate teaching (many years ago), I was told about the Yerkes–Dodson law. This law proposes an inverted U-shaped curve illustrating the relation between stress and learning (see Figure 8.1). In other words, learning is best when stress is at a moderate level. This creates motivation to learn. Low levels of stress are associated with low motivation, but high levels of stress cause anxiety that interferes with the learning process.

As far as brain function is concerned, the hippocampus plays a part here. Because the hippocampus is placed close to the amygdala, it is easily influenced by emotion. When stressed, the individual will be

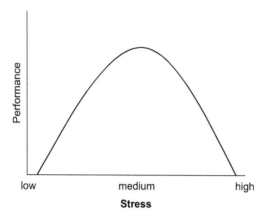

Figure 8.1 The Yerkes–Dodson curve, illustrating the relation between stress and learning.

experiencing heightened activity in the amygdala. This in turn affects memory processing that is taking place in the hippocampus. The ability to learn is thus reduced because of the close connection between these key sites in the brain. Some studies have shown that the amygdala actually becomes enlarged as a result of stressful experiences. This then means that it is more difficult for the controlling effect of the prefrontal cortex to operate and calm things down.

In Chapter 4, I discussed the notion of executive function, and the four elements associated with this, namely working memory, inhibition, resisting interference and flexibility. Recent research has shown how stress can inhibit executive function as a result of the release of stress hormones such as cortisol. These substances prepare the individual for a response to threat. Oxygen is directed to the muscles, in the visual cortex the eyes become focused on possible danger and so on. However, in dealing with threat, the brain directs the body's resources away from areas to do with executive function such as memory, resisting interference, flexibility and so on. It is in this way that stress reduces the learning capacity.

Some writers (e.g. Immordino-Yang and Gotleib, 2020) have pointed to the importance of meaning in understanding an individual's response to stress. Take, for example, two students about to do an identical maths test. One student has always done well in maths. She is alert and looking forward to the test. She may feel a small amount of stress, as she does not know how well she will do, but the test does not represent a major stress for her. For her, the test means a challenge but not a threat.

For the second student, however, this is a completely different experience. She has always struggled with maths, and she does not get on well with the teacher. She is worried about her ability to manage the test. For her, this test represents a significant degree of stress. As a result, stress hormones are released, and the amygdala becomes hyperactive. As she rehearses her fears and anxieties before she gets to the test, she is using up working memory resources, thus leading to a reduced capacity to perform well.

Stress can be experienced in many different ways, and, of course, individuals differ in their capacity to deal with stress. Learning is affected by stress, with some degree of stress having a positive influence on the learning process. The higher the level of stress, however, the greater the interference with learning. Stress can be cumulative, and it is important to understand how different stresses interact with each other. In Chapter 10, I outline how a greater understanding of stress can help students with their performance in class.

Stress and mental health

It is time now to turn to the question of whether stress and associated conditions, such as anxiety and depression, have increased over time. This is, of course, a subject of considerable public debate. It is also a question that is not so easy to answer, since we need high-quality research, using the same methods, over a period of time, in order to obtain reliable answers. The UK Government carried out major studies of mental health in children and young people in 1999 and 2004, but there was then a gap until, in 2017, another major study took place. Thus, the results that we do have are not exactly ideal.

As can be seen from the data in Figure 8.2, in 2017, approximately 14% of young people between the ages of 11 and 16 had a mental health condition (Hagell and Shah, 2019). At this age, there was little difference between boys and girls, but this altered in the older age group, with girls showing much higher levels of disorder. Up to the age of 16, behaviour problems are more common in boys, while emotional problems such as anxiety and depression are more common in girls. In the older groups, emotional problems are the most common symptoms for both sexes.

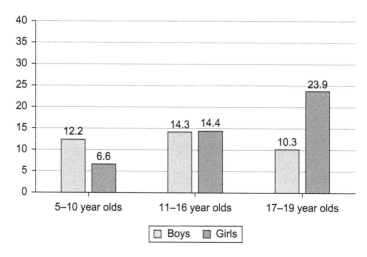

Figure 8.2 Percentage of children and young people with mental disorders, by age and sex, in England in 2017. (Hagell, A and Shah, R (2019) *Key Data on Young People 2019*. The Association for Young People's Health.)

Turning now to the question of change over time, data displayed in Figure 8.3 goes some way to answer this (Hagell and Shah, 2019). We can see that there has been some increase in disorders since 1999, although this increase is hardly dramatic. Figures are not available for the older age group (the 17–19-year-olds), since these data were not collected in the years 1999 and 2004.

It is very difficult to assess quite what lies behind the increase in disorders. It may be that there has been better reporting or more awareness of mental health issues over this time period. Another possible explanation is that mental health services have been cut, especially during the period of "austerity" from 2010 onwards. Reduced access to services will inevitably lead to more distress. Longer waiting times to get appointments at CAMHS services, combined with a reduction in local community services, will be bound to affect levels of mental health problems in this age group.

Looking at more specific problems, the study looked at self-harm rates for the 11–16-year age group. Here it was reported that 7.3% of girls had reported some form of self-harm, while boys had a lower rate with 3.1% reporting such behaviour. Self-harm is of course of particular concern for schools, so it is interesting to see that the overall level of this behaviour remains relatively low. Another important

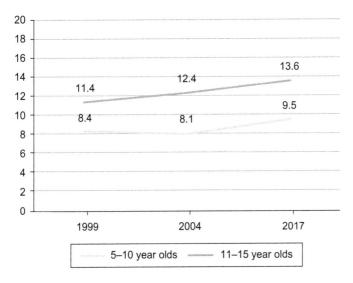

Figure 8.3 Time trends in mental disorders in 5–10-year-olds and 11–15-year-olds from 1999 to 2017. (Hagell, A and Shah, R (2019) *Key Data on Young People 2019*. The Association for Young People's Health.)

finding was the overlap between physical and mental health problems. A quarter of those with mental health problems also had a life-limiting long-term illness such as diabetes, epilepsy or asthma.

Another issue that is pertinent to the classroom is ADHD. This disorder, characterised by impulsivity, hyperactivity and inattention, is thought to be associated with poor inhibitory mechanisms in the brain. Readers will remember that inhibition is one of the features of executive function, and the ability to exercise inhibition is essential to concentrate and pay attention.

In Chapter 1, I talked about the role of synapses, and the fact that they have an on and off function. I talked of the signalling system in the brain as similar to an air-traffic control system, with this signalling system allowing the individual to concentrate on some incoming stimuli and block out others in order to concentrate. It is suggested that in those with ADHD this signalling system is not working as well as it should.

The most common approach in helping those with ADHD is to prescribe a medication such as Ritalin. This is one of the slow-acting psychostimulants and is thought to stimulate hormones such as dopamine in order to increase arousal and cognitive flexibility. In recent times, different approaches have been discussed that do not depend on medication. These include aerobic exercise, as well as other classroom-based activities that enable those with ADHD to develop inhibitory skills (see Thomas et al., 2020).

Other writers have also identified alternative approaches to ADHD. Howard-Jones (2010) suggests that the application of cognitive and behavioural approaches to managing the behaviour of students can be helpful, as can the involvement of parents and teachers in these techniques. This author also points to studies showing that increasing the agency of young people identified as having ADHD can really make a difference. In one study, students were asked how they felt about being labelled in this way. They talked of feeling "like a square peg in a round hole", with rigid requirements that were impossible for them to meet. Environments that are adaptable and flexible, and which offer support for these students, can make all the difference.

Autistic spectrum condition

I want to turn now to the topic of autism. This is one of the topics that is often high on the agenda for parents and teachers when thinking about brain development. Readers will note that I have called this section autistic spectrum condition (ASC), rather than autistic spectrum disorder (ASD). Many writers now take the view that autism in all its many aspects is not a disorder and it is important to move away from this concept. A recent article by one of the leading commentators on this condition, Simon Baron-Cohen, was entitled: "Neurodiversity: A revolutionary concept for autism and psychiatry" (Baron-Cohen, 2017).

The term "neurodiversity" is an important one, as it points to the fact that we all have brains that function differently. Autism is a condition in which the brain may be wired in a different way but is not necessarily defective. In my own reading on this subject, the book *Neurotribes* (Silberman, 2015) opened my mind to a new way of thinking about autism, and it is a book that I strongly recommend to readers.

It is important to recognise that when we speak of ASC, we may be referring to a very wide range of symptoms. Those with this condition can range from having no functional language and severe developmental delay to those with what is still called Asperger's syndrome, who have at least average intelligence and no history of language delay. What those with ASC have in common includes social communication difficulties, difficulties with cognitive empathy (sometimes called theory of mind) and difficulties adjusting to unexpected change. However, autism is also associated with cognitive strengths, such as excellent attention to detail, an excellent memory for detail and the ability to synthesise or detect patterns. It should also be acknowledged that some with this condition have remarkable talents. In his book *Neurotribes*, the author documents the life stories of some truly inspiring individuals

As far as brain development is concerned, it is clear that the brains of those with ASC do function differently from those in the wider population. However, in spite of numerous studies on this topic, there is little evidence to show that those with this condition have an actual brain disorder. Baron-Cohen (2017) summarises the current research. He points out that, as far as brain structure is concerned, there are some differences in the brains of those with ASC. It appears that the amygdala is slightly larger in childhood, and some sections of the corpus callosum (the bridge between the two hemispheres) are smaller.

Studies using brain imaging also show some differences. On some tasks, those with ASC show less brain activity than other young people, while on other tasks, they show greater activity in certain areas of the brain. These differences reflect some of the well-known behavioural differences, such as extra sensitivity to certain stimuli, or greater attention to detail. Baron-Cohen sums up the research in this way:

> Overall, the fMRI (scanning) evidence can be interpreted in terms of difference (the autistic brain is processing detail differently), and disability (e.g. the well-established theory of mind difficulties in autism are accompanied by neural differences) but again, no clear signs of disorder.
>
> (Baron-Cohen, 2017, p. 745)

In conclusion, it is evident that the brains of those with ASC are not necessarily defective. Thus, the term neurodiversity is more appropriate when we think about this condition, and there is a huge diversity in the ways that our individual brains function. If we recognise this, we move from seeing autism as a disorder to recognizing that everyone's brains are different.

Childhood trauma

Following training workshops that I have carried out with professional adults, one of the most common questions that I am asked has to do with childhood trauma and its impact on brain development during the teenage years. Understandably, those who work with young people who have experienced abuse or other traumatic events during their childhood want to know what effect these experiences will have on the teenage years. In particular, they want to know whether trauma will continue to affect brain development and whether it is possible for teenagers to recover from earlier traumatic experiences.

Of course, these are not easy questions to answer. There is such a wide variety of possible traumas that can impact on a child's life that it is hard to construct studies that provide conclusive answers. Nonetheless, many investigators have been studying this topic over the past decade or so. McRory and others at University College London (McRory et al., 2017) carried out a review of numerous studies on this topic. These authors conclude that there are significant differences in brain function of young people who have been exposed to childhood maltreatment.

These authors looked at evidence relating to four domains of brain function: threat processing, reward processing, emotion regulation and executive function. They reported that studies do illustrate differences in neural functioning in samples of young people who have experienced maltreatment in childhood. As far as threat processing is concerned, the evidence shows both heightened and depressed reactivity. This is thought to reflect either avoidance or hyper-vigilance.

Reward processing is seen to be blunted in comparison with other groups of young people, reflecting low expectations of positive experiences. Emotion regulation is significantly affected, with extra effort required to make sense of emotional stimuli. Finally, executive function is compromised, since this group finds it harder to recognise errors and utilise effective inhibitory mechanisms.

The authors use the term "latent vulnerability" to describe this overall picture of brain function. They explain this as a picture of brain activity that is adaptive in situations of trauma or maltreatment. The child develops a pattern of response that assists in dealing with the harmful environment. However, such a pattern of brain activity is not helpful as the individual moves away from an unsafe situation and is able to experience more nurturing and supportive relationships.

It should be noted that there are many challenges to this type of research. The great majority of studies have been carried out in the USA where definitions and criteria may be different from those we are used to in the UK. In addition, it is hard to find matched samples of children in order to draw sensible comparisons. As I have said, there are so many different types of adverse experience that might be said to include maltreatment. Lastly, many children who have experienced maltreatment have histories that include multiple placements and disrupted lives, so that studying these groups poses particular problems.

This leads on to the broader question of whether earlier trauma has a long-lasting impact on brain development. The simple answer to this is that we still do not know. However, there are some clues. First, it is the case that the human brain is amazingly plastic. This means that it has the capacity to repair itself. There are numerous examples of how, even after injury, the brain adapts and returns to normal functioning. There is also some useful information on this question from studies of fostering and adoption.

These studies show that the earlier the child is removed from the adverse environment, the more likely it is that the outcome will be a positive one. In addition, studies of resilience indicate that much will depend on the type of environment to which the child moves following maltreatment or trauma. The more supportive the environment, the more likely it is that the individual will overcome earlier adversity (for a very good summary, see Luthar, 2003).

There is much that we still do not know about the impact of childhood trauma. Nonetheless, there are some positive indications. The brain has a remarkable capacity to adjust and adapt. In addition, the environment plays a part. The more supportive the world around the child or young person, the greater the chance of being able to overcome earlier adversity.

Social media

As the range and impact of social media have increased in the recent past, so have the concerns and anxieties expressed by adults over the effect the virtual world has on the safety and mental health of young people. This is a huge topic and deserves much wider coverage, rather than a short section in a longer chapter. It hardly needs rehearsing that there are significant threats posed by the digital world, including such things as grooming, cyber-bullying, addiction to gaming, sexting and so on. However, it also has to be acknowledged that the virtual world has the most enormous potential for good.

Today, a world without the internet is hardly imaginable. This has become even more obvious as a result of the pandemic and the resulting lockdown in 2020/2021. For young people, the range of benefits is almost too wide to describe, ranging from communication, identity exploration, creativity, information gathering and so many other features of the online world. It will not be appropriate to explore these topics here in this short section. I will concentrate on one aspect of the subject, namely the possibility that accessing self-harm and suicide websites increases the risk of actual self-harm. This has become a topic of serious concern for parents and teachers alike.

Much publicity was given to the Molly Russell case in 2017. In this case, Molly, who was 14 at the time, very sadly took her own life, and her parents argued that the technology companies that own and curate these sites should take responsibility for Molly's suicide. The case has received wide publicity and has led to calls for more regulation in respect of social media content. A review by Hollis et al. (2020), entitled "Young people's mental health in the digital age" includes an excellent study by Lavis and Winter (2020) that sets out to provide some answers to this vexed question.

These authors collected data from thousands of posts on Instagram, Twitter and Reddit, as well as interviewing a large sample of young people who had experienced mental health problems. They conclude that it is very unlikely that an individual would be motivated to harm themselves simply as a result of looking at such websites or receiving messages concerning self-harm or suicide. In the view of these authors, what is most likely to happen is that self-harming behaviour is already occurring when the individual starts exploring the online world of self-harm.

The authors report endless examples of young people who use websites to learn more about the behaviour they are already engaged in, gather support from others who are experiencing similar depressive feelings or find out how to access therapeutic help. As the authors put it, the "contagion" model simply does not align with the facts. It is also of great interest to learn that many young people say that they turn to websites following conflict with parents or carers.

The authors review many examples of teenagers who disclose their self-harming behaviour to the adults close to them, only to be met by anger, disapproval or even disbelief. Under such circumstances, when young people in distress feel rejected by adults, they turn to the internet as an alternative source of information and assistance.

The conclusion here is that blaming the technology giants may provide an outlet for the feelings of the adults concerned, but it will be of limited help to young people. Of greater significance will be a move to provide better information about mental health to parents and teachers, as described in Chapters 9 and 11. The internet is here to stay, and the very best we can do is help young people navigate it safely. This is also a call for improved mental health services for this age group. Such services have become severely restricted in recent years, and if more resource could be directed to these services, young people would have less need to use the internet for information and support.

Conclusion

I am going to conclude this chapter by briefly considering the implications of Covid-19. In writing this book in the summer of 2020, I am conscious that we have been living through a most extraordinary time, when the mental health of young people may have been very much affected by their experiences in lockdown and the restrictions that have followed. There are many studies, ongoing at present, which are investigating the impact of Covid-19 on the mental health of the teenage population. However, at the time of writing, it is still too early to report on the findings of high-quality, large-scale studies. We remain dependent on very limited information at this point in time. A further lockdown in 2021 has added to the difficulties for young people. While we are still without good research on the impact of the pandemic on the mental health of teenagers, there seems little doubt that Covid-19 will have a significant effect on the lives of young people for some time to come.

Some tentative conclusions can be suggested, however, as a result of early research on this topic The first thing to say is that there has been a wide diversity of experiences. There is no doubt that during the first lockdown in 2020 some young people experienced improved well-being. There are three reasons for this. First, teenagers were able to get a better quality of sleep, many continuing to sleep late into the morning. Second, the stress related to school attendance was relieved. As I noted at the beginning of the chapter, the main stressors for teenagers do appear to be issues related to school. Having those stresses removed has led to a reduction in worry and anxiety. Lastly, the conflict between parent and teenager over screen time has also been removed. Since so much of life in lockdown has been shifted to the online world, this conflict has reduced or disappeared.

On the other hand, it seems likely that, for some, the experiences of the summer of 2020 did lead to an increase in mental health problems. Those living in cramped circumstances, with limited access to open spaces, have had a difficult time. There has been an increase in domestic violence and an increase in teenage aggressive behaviour towards parents and carers. It seems probable that those with pre-existing mental health problems have struggled too, especially since access to therapeutic services has been severely restricted during this period. It will be some time before the full picture emerges of the impact of Covid-19 on the mental health of young people. At the time of writing we do not yet know at what point in 2021 young people will be able to return to school. The continuation of lockdown into a second year, and the resulting uncertainty about the future for examinations, of entry into further or higher education, and for employment prospects cannot but add to an increase in levels of stress for this generation of young people.

In this chapter, I have covered a range of topics to do with stress and mental health. Some of the topics will inevitably have been covered in summary form. The links with our knowledge about the brain are clear in some cases, as, for example, with stress or with childhood trauma. In other cases, such as with the digital world, I have not tried to set out links with knowledge about the brain. I have included these topics as I believe they are of interest to readers and are directly relevant to the world of education.

Further reading

Frydenberg, E (2019) *"Adolescent coping: Promoting resilience and wellbeing: 3rd edition"*. Routledge, Abingdon, Oxon.
Howard-Jones, P (2010) *"Introducing neuro-educational research: Neuroscience, education and the brain"*. Routledge, Abingdon, Oxon.
Jensen, F (2015) *"The teenage brain: A neuroscientist's survival guide to raising adolescents and young adults"*. Harper, New York.
Luthar, S (2003) *"Resilience and vulnerability"*. Cambridge University Press, Cambridge.
Ogden, T and Hagen, K (2019) *"Adolescent mental health: Prevention and intervention"*. Routledge, Abingdon, Oxon.
Silberman, S (2015) *"Neurotribes: The legacy of autism and the future of neurodiversity"*. Avery Publishing, London.
Thomas, M, Mareschal, D and Dumontheil, I (Eds.) (2020) *"Educational neuroscience: Development across the life span"*. Routledge, Abingdon, Oxon.

References

Baron-Cohen, S (2017) "Neurodiversity: a revolutionary concept for autism and psychiatry". *Journal of Child Psychology and Psychiatry*. Volume 58. Pages 744–748.

Hagell, A and Shah, R (2019) *"Key data on young people 2019"*. The Association for Young People's Health. www.youngpeopleshealth.org.uk

Hollis, C, Livingstone, S and Sonuga-Barke, E (2020) "Special issue: young people's mental health in the digital age". *Journal of Child Psychology and Psychiatry*. Volume 61. Pages 837–940.

Immordino-Yang, M and Gotlieb, R (2020) Understanding emotional thought can transform educators' understanding of how students learn. In "Educational neuroscience: development across the lifespan". Thomas, M, Mareschal, D and Dumontheil, I (Eds.) Routledge. Abingdon, Oxon. Pages 244–270.

Lavis, A and Winter, R (2020) "Online harms or benefits? An ethnographic analysis of peer support around self-harm on social media". *Journal of Child Psychology and Psychiatry*. Volume 61. Pages 842–854.

McRory, E, Gerin, M and Viding, E (2017) "Childhood maltreatment, latent vulnerability, and the shift to preventative psychiatry: the contribution of functional brain imaging". *Journal of Child Psychology and Psychiatry*. Volume 58. Pages 338–357.

Chapter 9

The teenage brain for teachers
Planning a workshop

Introduction

One teacher said to me, after a workshop on the teenage brain:

> "I go to myself: 'Oh my god! How did I not know this stuff?' It is so interesting".

It is very rewarding to hear teachers react in this way after coming to one of my workshops. However, not everyone will respond with such enthusiasm! In designing a workshop on this topic there are a number of challenges. The first has to do with the expectations of teachers. What are they looking for when they sign up for a workshop on the teenage brain? In what way is this information going to help them with their day-to-day work with pupils?

One of the significant debates among educationalists has been to do with whether knowledge about the brain can be helpful or useful in the classroom setting. It has been assumed that when teachers imagine learning about the brain, they will expect it to help them with lesson planning, curriculum design or behaviour management. It is assumed that these are the topics that are high on their list of priorities.

In Chapter 1, I already referred to some of the concerns that were expressed by those in the field of education.

Thomas et al. (2019) wrote:

> It is worth pointing out why the goal of the field (neuroscience and education) is a challenging one. First, the way the brain learns is complex. Second, learning is only one part of education. Third, society's goals for education are not necessarily clear. And fourth, even for psychology, successful translation from science to educational practice has proved difficult.

(p. 479)

Although I understand the concerns of academics that knowledge of the brain will not translate into something useful in schools, I believe this is a misunderstanding. When coming to a workshop about the teenage brain teachers do not imagine they are going to get useful tips about curriculum design. They are clear that this information is going to help them understand their students. In the questionnaire I give out before the workshop I ask: "Could you identify three things concerning the teenage brain that you would like to know more about?" Here are some typical answers.

- "Why are teenagers moody?"
- "Why can they be so inconsistent and unpredictable?"
- "How can we get through to a student who is in a heightened emotional state?"
- "Why do teenagers seem to mature at different rates?"
- "How can we help as teachers with their tiredness?"
- "I would like to know more about influences, and how to navigate through them with the positives"
- "How old will they be when their brain is fully developed for reasoning?"

There are questions here about the rate of development, moods and emotions, sleep and tiredness and the impact of the peer group and other influences on behaviour. It will be clear to readers that what is being asked here has to do with having a better understanding of their students. This is the key for them. There seems little doubt that, for most, this knowledge can really make a difference in their work. As one trainer put it when talking to me about her workshops:

When I delivered the Teen Brain stuff to all the teaching staff, they said it made them think differently about the students. They were very positive about it. It made them think differently, so that when pupils got frustrated, perhaps finding it difficult to focus, or to focus on learning over longer periods, it made them think about doing shorter sharper activities. They also began to think about rewards and praise, and how we can make sure that pupils are more engaged across the whole curriculum So that was really helpful. And it helps people to understand that this is real, there is a genuine science behind it – that makes a big difference.

Learning and memory, or well-being?

From the earliest stages of this work, I have had to engage in the debate about whether the point of this training is to improve well-being and mental health, or whether it is about a better understanding of adolescent development. When we first delivered the workshop to practitioners in Hertfordshire (see Chapter 3), we were asked to include material on risk and resilience. The argument was advanced that this training could bring down the level of mental health problems in the county. It would do this by showing social workers and other professionals how to reduce risk and enhance resilience in the most vulnerable young people.

This was always going to be an aspiration rather than a concrete objective. The evaluations indicated that participants were getting a huge amount from the workshops. However, this was more to do with a general understanding of teenagers rather than a toolkit for improving mental health.

Typical comments from the evaluations bear this out.

- "It has enabled me to explain to teenagers how their brains develop, and why that matters for them"
- "Made me stop and think, and re-word what I say to young people I work with"
- "I use it to help teenagers understand that they are not alone, and it's happening to everyone"
- "Has helped me understand some of the behaviours of young people, and so have adjusted my practice".

As far as training for teachers is concerned, the dilemma has always been how to balance the different aims of a workshop. There is no doubt that emotional health and well-being remains a key concern for all schools. Yet I wanted the workshops to address educational matters too. I remain of the belief that a basic understanding of brain development has broad relevance for teachers. The content thus covers as wide a range of topics as can possibly be squeezed into one workshop session. There is certainly an argument that more should be included on mental health, but that has to be the subject of a second workshop. This is a dilemma that crops up again in Chapter 10 when I face the question of what to include in a lesson for pupils.

What do teachers know?

A further challenge relates to how much teachers already know. In much of the work I do with teachers, I frequently feel uncertain as to how much background they have in relation to the teenage brain. As part of the questionnaire I use at the beginning of the workshop, I include the question: "Could you identify three things that you know about the teenage brain?" Here are some answers.

Teacher 1
- Hormones can cause a huge effect on the brain
- They have a part of the brain that shuts off, causing them not to understand consequence
- The brain can be overloaded with emotions.

Teacher 2
- The brain is developing
- The development can lead to what is called "irrational" behaviour
- Often impulse becomes the greater drive leading to risky behaviour.

Teacher 3
- Continually developing
- Different parts of the brain develop at different rates
- Easier to make memories/recall if you learn later in the day.

Teacher 4
- Change in hormones
- It is still developing up to the age of 25
- It is fascinating!

I am, of course, just selecting a small sample to give the reader a sense of the sorts of responses I have been getting. These are hugely helpful to me as a trainer and they have formed the basis for the content of my workshops. There is no point in covering information that is already familiar. On the other hand, the topics identified make it clear that there are broad notions held by teachers that need further explanation.

Most are aware that the brain continues to develop, but few know exactly what that involves. Everyone recognises that there is an impact on the management of emotions, but it will be evident that there is much more to be said on this topic. All teachers know that there is a greater chance of risky behaviour during the teenage years. Yet, risk is a complex notion, and a lot more has been learnt about this in recent years. It is also the case that many topics are not mentioned by the great majority of teachers. To take some examples, most know little about pruning or how the two halves of the brain work together, the role of hormones such as dopamine and recent sleep research.

The question facing anyone designing a workshop for teachers is how to build on existing knowledge, while also creating a sense of excitement and interest in new information? I should say that some of the material is the same as I would present in any workshop, whether for students, parents or professionals. This is the basic introduction to the key changes that are taking place, as well as some explanations of how these changes impact on behaviour. However, it is also the case that certain topics – learning and memory for example – will be of greater relevance for teachers than for other groups.

I will briefly outline the content of the workshop I have been using for teachers. More about the workshop will be found in Appendix 2, and the actual slides are to be found on the accompanying website (www.routledge.com/cw/coleman).

The Workshop

- *Some background* (the history of scanning, changing views of the teenage brain and the importance of new knowledge)
- *The key changes* (development of various parts of the brain, the importance of pruning and hormone variation)
- *How to understand maturity* (faster processing and greater connectivity between two sides of the brain)
- *Learning and executive function* (types of learning, changes in the brain as a result of learning, the meaning of executive function and how this links with classroom performance)
- *Hormones and reward processing* (how hormone levels vary in adolescence, key hormones such as dopamine and serotonin and why rewards are especially important for teenagers)
- *The social brain* (why the peer group matters and learning about social skills, alongside a greater focus on how the individual appears to others, leading to "preoccupation with the self" and "egocentrism")
- *Sleep* (the role of melatonin, the impact of sleeping later in teenagers, memory consolidation in sleep, sleep deficit and its impact on learning and how to get into good sleep routines)
- *Healthy brain development* (the importance of the environment, facilitating the development of the prefrontal cortex, providing good support for students, finding ways to reduce stress and getting oxygen to the brain).

Practical gains for the school

In the interviews I carried out, I always asked what the practical gains for the school could be in offering teachers more training about the teenage brain. While everyone recognised the pressures on teachers, most of the people I talked to had little doubt that more information on this topic would be of benefit to the wider school environment. One teacher put it like this:

> Anything that improves understanding of the young people we are working with must be a gain. Understanding is the best way to move forward. I believe this is a huge step forward. Before I did the course I didn't really understand how students are changing. Knowing about the changes in their brains, it can only be positive. We are in this to educate people, and this can educate us. We have to get that knowledge and build on it.

Many teachers mentioned the fact that they had not realised how much change is happening in the brain. This seemed to be one of the key facts that could really make a difference in how teachers respond to their students.

> One thing I found particularly powerful – knowing that it is the years of puberty that are so significant. For the teens who have had a disadvantaged start, they feel that they are behind and never going to catch up. So, ideas about the changing brain can be very empowering.

This knowledge can also be a motivating force helping teachers to recognise the potential for change. Quite a few of my interviewees talked about the way knowledge about the brain could alter the way teachers view their students.

> It is important to bring it out, that things are changing, it is not all set. For teachers here, well, they think a pupil is not doing so well, and they just don't think things can change. We do want to give everyone the same chances. We do always want for teachers to **not** feel – what's the point? This pupil is already in a difficult situation. What can we do in school? But we can, and understanding that the brain is changing all the time is the key to it all.

Finally, there is the question of having a better understanding of the learning process. Knowledge about the brain is adding to a broader awareness of how we all learn new material. This is absolutely central to the work of every teacher. If this information can be made available to those in education, it can only be of huge benefit to students and teachers alike.

People like it when it is researched, and practical, and feeds so clearly into what we are all doing. It is about how students can learn better. Teachers need to know this, we need to keep talking about it, keep sharing these ideas, that the teenage brain is changing and developing It should be part of teacher training, no doubt about it.

The impact on students? I think they get short-changed, I really do. I think teenagers get a bit of a raw deal, they are really misunderstood. [They] feel that, they actually know that. Understanding of the teen brain helps you to show more empathy to young people. If we as adults show them more empathy you get that back in return. I do honestly feel that it would help them feel a bit better understood, perhaps respected a bit more.

During this project, I have learnt how positive it can be for teachers to have more information about teenage brain development. There seems little doubt that this knowledge changes the way those in secondary education view their students. It can provide an exciting and invigorating insight into adolescent development. In this way, it has the potential to alter teacher motivation and enhance teacher confidence. I believe this should become a required element in teacher training and all continuing professional development.

Reference

Thomas, M, Ansari, D and Knowland, V (2019) "Educational neuroscience: progress and prospects". *Journal of Child Psychology and Psychiatry.* Volume 60, Number 4, Page 479.

Chapter 10

The teenage brain for students
A lesson plan

Introduction

If the challenges in constructing a workshop for teachers were significant, the questions surrounding a lesson plan for students were even more pressing! How was this material to fit into the curriculum? For which year groups would it be most suitable? What content would have the greatest appeal? How to interest students in this new knowledge?

The initiative for this work came from the practitioners attending the "My Teen Brain" sessions in Hertfordshire (see Chapter 3). At the end of the day, the question was always raised by one or more participants. "This is great, and very valuable for us in our work, but what about telling young people themselves about this stuff?"

Discussions with teachers frequently came to the same point. Most professional adults could see that a better understanding of brain development would be helpful for all young people. It was an exciting moment when the commissioners in Hertfordshire agreed to provide funding for some exploratory work. They wanted to see if it would be possible to design a suitable lesson plan.

Rationale

For this project to be effective, it was going to be necessary to have a clear rationale. However, this was not as easy as it first appeared. Different stakeholders had varying beliefs about the potential value of lessons for students on the teenage brain. Discussions in the early meetings circled around questions like this:

- Is it to teach science?
- Is it to help young people understand themselves better?

- Is it to give them strategies to manage their lives better, such as getting into better sleep routines?
- Is it to reduce mental health problems?
- Is it to reduce risk-taking behaviour?

The planning team did not want to rule out any of these objectives, apart from the teaching of science. The view was taken that these materials might be complementary to GCSE Biology, for example, but they should not be developed as a science lesson. Most people on the team argued that the best place for this material was going to be in a PSHE lesson, as this was understood by most secondary schools in Hertfordshire. From my perspective, there was no way I could deliver all the objectives in one lesson. There would have to be some focus and the setting of some priorities.

It was important to find out what the students themselves thought about this. In discussions with those in Years 9 and 10, it was clear that the topics most prominent on their list of priorities were revision, exams and stress. When asked what they would like to know more about some typical answers were as follows:

- "How your brain can cope with revision and remember information"
- "How the brain recovers past memories and how that affects your choices/decisions"
- "How different parts work, what they do, and how they affect the body"
- "To help us with our GCSEs, and to know how to revise. How our memory works"
- "What happens during exams, and when you are stressed?"

It was evident from our discussions that emotional health and wellbeing were high on the list of priorities for commissioners. However, it was going to be difficult to cover all the possible topics in only one lesson. As with the workshops for teachers, I believed that it was essential to include a general introduction to the changes taking place in the brain. I also wanted to address the question of revision and explain a little about learning and memory.

Some key questions

While planning this I had a number of questions at the forefront of my mind. First and foremost was how to design a lesson that would provide useful information for the students at the same time as being really interesting and engaging. I was also exercised about how this lesson would become embedded in the curriculum and who would deliver it. It was clear that a considerable amount of piloting would have to take place before a final lesson plan could be rolled out.

Several other questions had to be answered. First, what would be the best stage for the introduction of these materials? While some thought that it would be good to deliver this as early as possible in the secondary curriculum, others argued that a certain degree of intellectual development would be necessary for students to make the best use of the information. The consensus was that Years 7 and 8 were probably too early, while Year 10 was taken up with GCSE preparations. In the end, most schools opted for Year 9 as the best time to deliver these materials.

One teacher said:

> Year 8 is a bit borderline. Some Year 8s might manage it, some wouldn't. In our school there are some who are a little bit on the immature side, so we would want to put it into Year 9.

Another said:

> Probably you want to get it quite early, but I wonder whether Year 8 might be too early? I think Year 8 may be a bit too early, but you want to get in early so that they can understand it as they go through it. Maybe Year 9 as they are more ready for it. They are going to be a bit more affected by it. They are more mature then, so Year 9 I think is best.

A second question had to do with whether one lesson was enough to cover the material. In the end, this was going to be very much determined by the flexibility that each school has in its approach to the curriculum. However, it was made clear to me that I should design a lesson plan for one lesson only, as this was the only way it was going to be acceptable to the broad range of schools. Having said this, I should stress that I was fortunate to work with some teachers who wanted to explore creative ways of delivering the material. Many teachers thought that more than one lesson was necessary and they were determined to find ways of finding space to do this. I was particularly impressed by one senior teacher who planned to run the materials over a whole week!

We think you have got to do a whole week on it. On Monday morning we do an introduction to it, on Tuesday we have sessions where we will keep popping it in, such as a questionnaire about the brain. Then on Wednesday we have an assembly, where we showed a model of a brain and we talked about the two sides of it. We also showed a little film. They liked that! We bookended this by two small sessions to go over it on Thursday and Friday. You've got to do a whole week on it with the whole year group, so that they can talk about the connections, what it all means for them. I must tell you we have only done a pilot project on it so far, we will see how it will work!

A third question that concerned me had to do with the following issue: who, in the school environment, would be willing to become ambassadors for these materials? And where would my lesson plan fit in the curriculum? I discussed this with many teachers at both senior and junior levels. Almost everyone agreed that a lesson on the teen brain, if it was to find a place in an already crowded curriculum, was going to be seen as part of PSHE. It followed that the teachers most likely to embrace this idea were going to be those tasked with teaching PSHE or some form of health education.

We do have a group of PSHE teachers – that is who we would see delivering this. Somebody who is well trained and has an idea of what they are talking about. There are elements, the more complex elements such as the intricacies of the brain, and the vocabulary as well, means that training would be necessary. The delivery's got to be really good. As long as the training is there other teachers could do it, but in reality for us it would definitely be PSHE teachers.

It could be in the wider curriculum. That is something we hear a lot about. But given that the new PSHE strategy is coming in in 2020, that is helpful, isn't it? A place now has to be made for this in the curriculum. It fits nicely, and a way has to be found for delivering this. People have to think about it, and find a way to get it in.

How to engage students?

There is no doubt that I went down a few dead ends in the early phases of this project. Although I sought advice from experienced teachers, there were no models for this project, nor were other trainers attempting to develop anything similar. I tried many different approaches. I developed a pack of cards with different ideas about the brain on each card. I used an app showing a picture of the brain that I downloaded to my iPad. Techniques like this simply did not work in a classroom setting.

As time went on, and as I had more time with small groups of students, I gradually evolved some exercises that seemed to be effective. The first breakthrough came when I realised that I had to get the students to tell me something about the changes, rather than me telling them! Did they know about brain changes? What did they think had changed since they became teenagers? From this followed the construction of what I have called the Change Questionnaire. I made it as simple as possible, taking eight topics and giving them a binary choice. For example, did they think they were more or less moody since they had become a teenager? Did they think their memory was better or worse? Was it easier or harder to get to sleep now? (The Change Questionnaire is in Appendix 1.)

I chose the topics carefully so that the answers would be easily linked to the materials on the brain. I have collected over 500 responses, so I can be fairly confident that I now know how a broad cross-section of young people will respond. In my sample, 89% of responses said they were moodier since they had become a teenager, 95% found life more stressful and 80% found it harder to get to sleep. These three topics are the ones that show the clearest trends. However, 73% of responses said they would be more inclined to take risks as a teenager and the majority said that their memory was better and their scientific reasoning improved. The other results are shown in Appendix 1.

The results for the three topics of stress, moods and sleep are especially useful, as each can be linked to aspects of brain development. Therefore, teachers can pick up the threads and highlight how the lesson is going to go on and explore these topics further. I should add that there is potential here for further discussion and learning. Why are so many students experiencing stress? Is this a part of adolescent development or is it to do with exams, tests and pressure from teachers? Is it to do with the peer group? With social media? Or are there other stressors that students want to mention?

In fact, all the topics can be used to lead on to further discussion, whether it is to do with memory, risk, sleep, talking to parents and so on. However, there are also significant time pressures if the content of the lesson is to be covered in the space of 45 minutes. Teachers will have to make their own decisions about how to manage the material. It is important to note that most teachers who have attended the training workshops have agreed that, if possible, they would want to take more than one lesson to cover these materials.

While the Change Questionnaire worked well, I still wanted something to introduce the lesson, something that would really get the students thinking about the brain. For this purpose, I developed a true or false set of questions. These can be read out to the class and students can be encouraged to participate by a show of hands. Examples include: "When we go to sleep our brain goes to sleep too" (false) and "The brain is in two halves with a bridge in the middle" (true). I have always found that, no matter how sleepy or unresponsive the group appears at first, almost all students do engage with such a task. Again, topics covered in these true or false statements are designed to link with topics that will appear later in the lesson. Of course, teachers can make up their own statements if they so wish.

The lesson plan

There are seven parts to the lesson plan. There are both tutor and student packs (again, these can be found in the accompanying website www.routledge.com/cw/coleman).

- Part 1 – Learning objectives (the purpose of the lesson for the students, or "what is this all about?")
- Part 2 – The brain (showing a simple model of the brain, highlighting key areas such as the prefrontal cortex)
- Part 3 – The true or false quiz
- Part 4 – Change in the teenage years (identifying the main changes, including maturation, connectivity, upheaval as a result of pruning and alteration of the hormone balance). Part 4 also includes the introduction of the Change Questionnaire and subsequent discussion
- Part 5 – Learning and memory (how the brain works, how memories are formed, an optional exercise on memory, points about revision and sleep and its role in memory consolidation)
- Part 6 – Stress and emotion (the amygdala, links between the brain and strong emotions, the role of hormones and an exercise about managing stress)
- Part 7 – Conclusion (underlining that the brain and the environment interact and that there are things that students can do to help with healthy brain development).

Broader benefits for the school

I will conclude with some thoughts about how the introduction of this lesson plan might benefit the wider objectives of the school. As noted in Chapter 9, there are clearly benefits for teachers. These benefits relate to teachers having a better understanding of the changes experienced by their students, as well as knowing more about the learning process.

I also talked to those I interviewed about the benefits for the students themselves. Most believed there to be a number of possible benefits in the introduction of these materials. These were to do both with improving learning skills as well as helping students understand themselves better. Such thoughts fitted nicely with the learning objectives set out for the students at the start of the lesson.

We said: "The work you are going to do in this lesson is designed to help you:

- Understand yourself and what is happening to you at this stage of your life
- Manage yourself better (your moods, feelings and relationships)".

Those I interviewed saw a strong link between a better understanding of oneself as a teenager and a greater commitment to learning and the educational goals of the school. Here is how one teacher expressed this thought:

> It's about how you learn better, and understand yourself better. A lot of students start doubting themselves. They have anxiety when we talk about the emotional side of it. They need to know that it impacts their decision making. And we can give them that confidence, maybe confidence is the wrong word, assurance maybe, that what they are going through may be tough, but it's not that they have a mental health condition. What they are going through is normal, basically, it's everyone. And we can help them with that.

Other people I interviewed talked more directly about educational goals. These teachers saw that having more of a perspective on their development could assist the student in the school setting.

> From an educational perspective it would help them access their education better. It would give them a bit more perspective on their behaviours. When they are thinking about doing something

in a particular way, or acting in a certain way, it helps them have a bit more perspective.

It could help with learning. We are a linear school, there is a lot of pressure on students to learn materials over two years, so anything we can do to help them retain that information is so useful. We need them to know about how to learn, and techniques that will help them. Also, we can tell them it could be a difficult time for your teenage brain at this moment, and so hopefully they could be a bit more on board with what we are trying to do.

From all those I spoke to there seemed little doubt that a lesson on the brain and the way it develops during the years of secondary school can have enormous benefits. Of course, many questions remain. Space has to be found in the curriculum, and teachers themselves have to commit to learning new material so they are confident in delivering the lesson. I am confident that, over the next few years, more information about brain development will become available. As a result, it will become increasingly obvious that this information must be an essential part of secondary education.

Chapter 11

The teenage brain for parents
Engaging families in new knowledge

Introduction

In order to deliver workshops for parents, it was clear that schools were going to be the most obvious places to locate these sessions. Many of the teachers and school nurses who attended the early "My Teen Brain" workshops in Hertfordshire identified parents as a group that could really benefit from this information. This was highlighted by the fact that many of those who attended these workshops were themselves parents of teenagers. Their comments on the evaluation forms indicated a high level of interest in these materials in relation to their own experiences of parenting.

Here are three comments indicating how professionals had made use of the workshop material.

- "It has helped me in my professional work, but in my personal life too. It has helped me to relate to my own teenagers differently. I find I can connect with them in a more empathic way"
- "The fact that thinking ahead/consequences is one of the last things to develop in a teen brain – this has been really helpful. I am much calmer now when dealing with anything that is a bit challenging!"
- "It has helped me understand that they are not just being awkward. Often, they may not have the rationale to understand what they have done. It enables language to be developed so that we can deal with things better at home".

From these comments, it was clear that "My Teen Brain" training would be helpful to parents. All who knew about the work were confident about this. However, there were numerous questions about how to work with schools and how to deliver this material in the most effective manner.

How to deliver these materials?

Much of my past work has had to do with running support groups for parents of teenagers. As a result, I am only too well aware of the challenges for parents of being able to attend such groups. There are a variety of reasons for this. Pressures of time, difficulties in arranging childcare and anxiety about being in some way exposed as an inadequate parent all play a part. Perhaps understandably, information sessions for parents run by the school in the evenings are often poorly attended. As a group, parents of teenagers are hard to engage.

In order for this project to be successful, it was going to be essential to identify schools that could see the benefits of this information. We would also need a group of practitioners within the community that could act as the link between myself as the trainer and the schools in the area. I have to thank the Early Help team at Bedford Borough Children's Services for encouraging me to develop these workshops and for showing so much enthusiasm for this work.

There were particular advantages in starting this work with Bedford Borough. It is a relatively small authority, with a total of 12 secondary schools. The Early Help Team had good relationships with all the schools. They also had a coherent team of trainers who were keen to become involved in this work. The question of sustainability was an important consideration. My time and capacity are limited. As with the work with students, I wanted to find a way to ensure that the delivery of the workshop could continue over time. The team at Bedford Borough offered this possibility and were keen to be trained to take on the work after I left.

The role of the school

The role of the school was going to be critical to the success of the project. The first school we chose had a particularly enthusiastic headteacher and staff who were on board with the project. However, they were also cautious, pointing out the low level of attendance at previous events for parents.

It was agreed that good publicity was going to be essential. There was also much discussion about the title and description of the workshop. We wondered about how to identify it as something that would be of interest to parents, without being at all threatening. A parental concern was that if they attend a workshop – for example on drugs – it would look as if their teenager had a problem with that issue. We had to identify this workshop on the brain as something that was of general interest and was not going to highlight anything to do with "teenage problems".

The first school that offered to run this workshop put a lot of energy into the publicity. They used social media and the local press, as well as sending all parents notices through the school email system. This undoubtedly paid off. The first plan was to use a room that would be suitable for up to 50 parents, as everyone agreed that if that number turned up it would be a success. In the event we had to change the venue twice, ending up in the large auditorium with 180 parents!

Some of the comments after this first workshop were as follows:

- "I felt it has empowered me with strategies to aid in my parenting"
- "It's made me re-assess the way I 'parent' my children"
- "I need to listen to my teenager more, and we need to have fun together. Light Bulb!"
- "I'm far more confident as a parent now. I think also my empathy towards my teens has also increased, hopefully resulting in less drama at home. Thank you"
- "Made me not feel such a 'parent failure'".

I should note that not all workshops in other schools have attracted such large numbers. There is no doubt that many factors contribute to take-up. Publicity is key, as well as the interest and commitment of teachers. However, as a general rule, we have found a significant degree of enthusiasm for these workshops. Large numbers of parents have attended in a variety of schools and evaluations have been similar to those noted previously.

An interactive workshop

While much of the material that would be used for parents was going to be the same as the material I developed for teachers and other professionals, there was going to be a challenge in designing it to be appropriate for a diverse group of parents. There were a number of objectives that I had in mind while developing these materials.

In the first place, I wanted to be sure that there would be lots of opportunities for parents to talk and share their experiences. I also wanted the workshops to feel like a safe space for any discussions that might take place. I recognised that in any group some parents might already know each other, while others might be reticent about sharing any information about their sons or daughters. Privacy and confidentiality are always going to be factors that have to be taken into consideration. It would be necessary to share some basic ground rules before the start of the workshop.

One of the things we know about parents of teenagers is that some do feel shame or guilt about what is happening at home. Teenagers are good at making parents feel bad about their parenting. In some families, there can be a constant refrain on the subject of how parents are ruining the teenager's life. I well remember one parenting group I ran when a mother came in saying: "I am here because I am being told that I am a crap parent!"

I decided to use some warm-up exercises to get people talking, as well as including slots during the workshop for small group chats. Ideally, the room would be set out with small tables, having a maximum of five or six parents at each table. It was notable that, in the example I gave previously with 180 parents, such an arrangement was impossible. Flexibility on the part of the trainer is essential! I was initially anxious as to how the arrangement of a large auditorium could work. However, getting parents to talk to those next to them seemed to be acceptable, and in this particular situation, parents were not reticent in asking questions or becoming involved in discussion with others.

A second important objective is to make the material accessible for a diverse group of parents. One group would be looking for general information about teenagers, while others might have specific concerns. We have had parents attend because their teenager was not eating or could not focus on schoolwork or had been diagnosed with one condition or another. These parents were looking for more information about that particular condition.

It is important to be clear from the start that these workshops are not designed for individual consultations. The trainer has to be sensitive to this. In the question-and-answer section of the workshop, time has to be allowed for parents to express their concerns. On the other hand, the workshop cannot be dominated by one or two parents with pressing needs. A balance has to be struck, and opportunities offered for such parents to receive extra support outside the workshop.

Thirdly, the content of the workshop has to be credible and thus based on science. Yet, it also has to be accessible for parents who themselves may not be highly educated. It was going to be important to design the workshop so that the materials were at the same time interesting, not too difficult to understand and useful in terms of the challenges of parenting teenagers. This was a considerable task! More detail about the workshop can be found in Appendix 2 and the slides and other guidance is available on the accompanying website (www.routledge.com/cw/coleman).

Content of the workshop

It was decided that a two-hour workshop in the evening was a sensible length of time that would seem acceptable to parents. Most schools ran the workshops from 6.00 to 8.00, with tea and coffee provided either before or afterwards. The content was divided into the following sections:

- Welcome, and setting out ground rules
- Exercises
- Teen brain material
- Small group discussions.

In relation to ground rules, it is best, if at all possible, to ask the group to suggest rules that will make them feel comfortable. Confidentiality is one suggestion that always comes up and is best explored a bit so that everyone knows what it means in that particular context. Other suggestions usually include things such as turning off phones, being respectful of others and emphasizing that "no questions is a silly question".

Moving on to the exercises, I wanted these to be activities that would prompt new thinking and signpost ideas that would be reflected in the material about the brain. I used three exercises.

Typical teenage behaviours

This first exercise requires participants to write down – using post-it notes or any other available paper – five typical teenage behaviours. Once they have done so they can either share their responses with others in their small groups or read out their answers to the whole group. Common answers include: "moody, sleepy, irritable, challenging, rude, funny, obsessed with their phones, silent, grumpy, always tired, a closed book". In most groups, the ratio is normally 90% negative answers and 10% positive statements. There are many ways that these answers can be used. First, it raises the question of how adults perceive teenagers. Second, most answers link to things that will feature as part of the material on the teenage brain.

Typical parenting behaviours, as your teenager would describe them

This requires participants to do the same, only focusing on their own parenting this time. This is a real eye-opener for many parents, as they have rarely liked to think about how they are perceived by their teenagers. Answers include things such as: "dictator, Genghis Khan, irritable, never satisfied, unfair, never there, doesn't listen, old-fashioned". The positive answers are even fewer in this exercise than in the first one. There is usually a lot of laughter during the course of this activity. The value of this is obvious since it allows the trainer to open discussions about how teenagers and parents perceive each other and how that affects relationships in the home.

The change questionnaire

This is the questionnaire discussed in the previous two chapters. More detail will be found in Appendix 1. In essence, it asks young people to say how they think they have changed since they became a teenager. In this instance, the activity involves asking parents to complete the questionnaire as they think their teenager would do so. The purpose of this is to get parents thinking about their teenager and imagining how they feel about growing and changing. The exercise allows for a discussion of moods, emotions, stress, sleep and various other aspects of the teenage experience.

As far as the Teen Brain material is concerned, this is very similar to that used in other workshops. However, the material is divided into short sections so that the session remains interesting and lively. The full detail of the workshop will be found in Appendix 2. In brief, the sections are as follows:

- Why this is important – it is a critical stage in development
- The key changes that take place in the teenage brain
- The role of hormones – dopamine, melatonin
- The positive things that arise from these changes – new skills, increased vocabulary
- The not-so-positive things – emotion regulation, risk behaviour

- The social brain – the role of the peer group, preoccupation with the self
- Sleep – the importance of this, what can be done to get into good sleep routines
- The brain and the environment interact, so parents have a big role to play.

Finally, I should mention the small group discussions. I see these as absolutely central to the impact of the workshop. Parents will get as much out of sharing ideas and experiences with other parents as they will from the actual content of the session. Trainers may wish to introduce their own subjects for discussion. I usually make sure that there is ample time for introductions, and at least two breaks when a topic for discussion is introduced. This could follow one of the exercises or it could be on an issue such as sleep, homework or social media.

Next steps

Since the initial development of the workshop in Bedford Borough, many other authorities and voluntary sector organizations have shown an interest in this work. I should particularly mention Family Links, the Charlie Waller Memorial Trust, Parenting Northern Ireland and Rollercoaster. All four organizations have embraced the concept and worked hard to roll out the workshop as widely as possible. As a result of Covid-19 and consequent lockdowns, there has been an explosion in the use of online teaching and training. This has created new opportunities to reach groups of parents that would have been unthinkable before the crisis of the pandemic.

One of the big challenges with the parent workshop, as well as the other workshops I have designed, has to do with training the trainers. How do you create a group of trainers who feel skilled and confident enough to run these workshops themselves? In Bedford Borough this was not a problem since there already existed a small and skilled group of trainers. Of course, this is not necessarily the case in other local authorities.

As well as designing the workshop for parents, it has been necessary to think about how to create a training package for those who wish to run the workshops and to offer the materials to a wider audience. This is a subject that is outside the scope of this book. However, further guidance on training the trainers will be found on my website (www.jcoleman.co.uk)

Implications for schools

I want to conclude this chapter by considering the implications for schools in introducing this workshop for the parents of their students. In the previous two chapters, I considered the wider benefits for the school of introducing workshops on the teen brain for teachers and students. References were made to both groups having a better understanding of the learning process. For students, it was seen to be a benefit if they were able to understand something about their own development. For teachers, it was agreed that it could be of great value to have an understanding about the degree of maturation in the brain, as well as a recognition that things were not set, but capable of change.

What about the benefits of workshops for parents? I believe there are three significant gains to be achieved through this process. The first is very similar to that identified for teachers and students. For parents to know more about teenage development and specifically about changes in the brain should lead to more confident parenting. This, in turn, helps to create a more collaborative relationship between parent and teacher. Not to mention, of course, the fostering of better relationships in the home.

> To have a 2-hour workshop for parents, for them to understand the key developmental stages of the teenage brain, it has been invaluable. They really need to understand what is happening, and the workshop is a really interactive experience. When they are dealing with the ups and downs of parenting, they know that their young person, their teenagers are going through these changes.

The second advantage relates to the anxieties of parents. A number of teachers expressed concern about the pressures placed on them by parents who believe there is something wrong with their son or daughter. Many talked about experiences they had with parents who thought their teenager was abnormal in some way.

> A lot of our parents and students are self-diagnosing themselves with mental health problems. As soon as a child is moody, frustrated, angry, fed up with the world, parents automatically look it up on line and they go: "Oh! My child has got a personality disorder", or something like that. They haven't been to a GP or anything. It is very difficult to persuade a parent that this is

normal. If we could do some sort of session for parents so that they could understand what is normal and what is not that would be brilliant.

Another teacher made the point in a different way:

I have been able to relay this information about the changes in the brain to anxious parents and to annoyed school staff to try to help them understand that the young person is being a "typical teen".

Finally, there is a debate about whether schools should be contributing to what might be called "parent education". Is this the role of the school? In my view, if it leads to students who are more engaged in education, and parents who have a better understanding of adolescent development, there can be little doubt that there are enormous gains in the provision of these workshops. As one team leader in the Early Help Service in Bedford Borough expressed it:

It has really changed the conversations that these parents are having with their teenagers, but also with teachers. It has just been invaluable. The main thing I always think is it changes people's language. I will give an example. I was recently in a meeting where a 13 year old boy had just come back from a temporary exclusion. The meeting was to think about what the consequences are, and what will happen next. Both the parent and the teacher had been on our training (the Teen Brain training), and the common language they both had was fantastic. They could talk about different parts of the brain, and what that meant. I was sitting back listening to what they had learnt. It was a much more targetted conversation. It changes how people think. I thought it was just amazing, a real rich conversation.

In this chapter, I have shown how the introduction of a workshop for parents on the teen brain can have benefits for all concerned. There is obvious value in providing this information for parents, but in addition, it is manifest that there are benefits for the school as well. Running such workshops is not without its challenges. It is essential to have commitment from school staff and ensure that sufficient publicity is provided before the workshop so that the numbers attending make it all worthwhile. It is necessary to have teachers or trainers available to take on the task of running the workshops professionally. From my experience, I am convinced this is entirely possible. There is a growing recognition that information about brain development can make a significant difference to the parenting of teenagers as well as to the education of students. I hope that what I have said in these chapters will foster more enthusiasm for this work.

Appendix I
"The Change Questionnaire"

As I have noted in various chapters of the book, I devised the Change Questionnaire while developing the lesson plan for students. One day I was standing in front of a class describing the changes in the brain, and I suddenly thought: "I wonder if anyone has actually asked these students what their experiences are of the changes since they became teenagers?"

With this in mind, I constructed the Change Questionnaire, a very simple exercise with binary choices. An example of a completed questionnaire can be seen in Chart A.1. In essence, the Questionnaire requires a yes or no answer: for example: "Is your memory better or worse since you became a teenager?" Students had no difficulty in completing the questionnaire and it was quick and easy to do.

I must emphasise that this is not a scientific study. The numbers of responses that are provided in Table A.1 simply reflect my experience of using this questionnaire with 510 students in approximately 20 secondary schools. The majority of students were in Year 9, but some Year 10 students were included as well. The sample is not large enough for me to break down the responses by age or gender. In any event, I was not able to standardise the process of administration since circumstances varied from school to school. Sometimes, my class was interrupted, and sometimes, I could not prevent the students from discussing their responses with others.

The main purpose of the Questionnaire was to introduce topics relating to the changes taking place in the brain. I asked students to raise hands if, for example, they had responded "More" when asked whether they felt more or less moody now that they were teenagers.

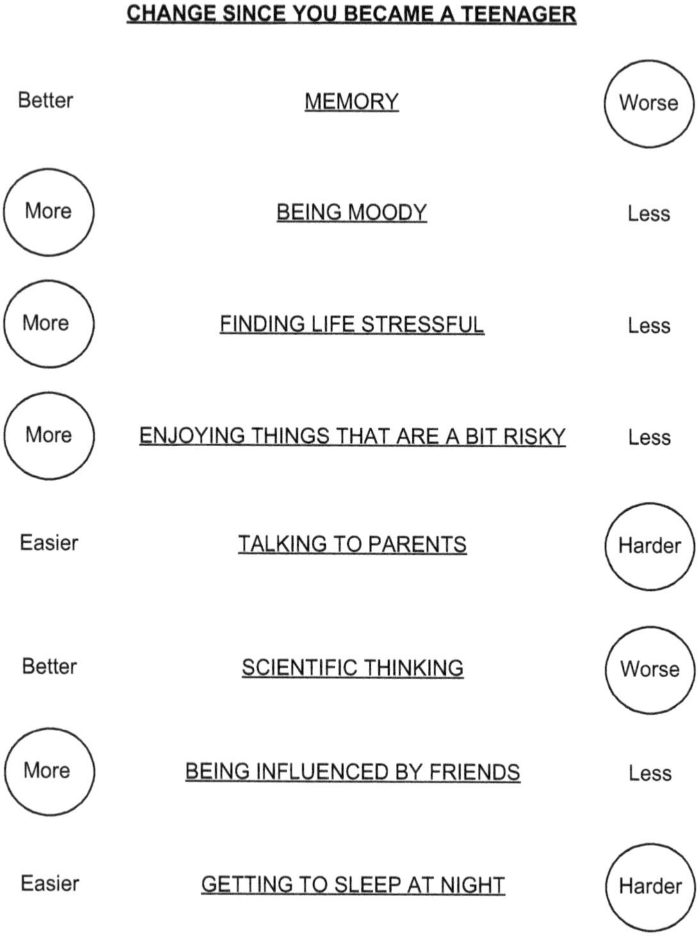

CHANGE SINCE YOU BECAME A TEENAGER

| Better | MEMORY | (Worse) |

| (More) | BEING MOODY | Less |

| (More) | FINDING LIFE STRESSFUL | Less |

| (More) | ENJOYING THINGS THAT ARE A BIT RISKY | Less |

| Easier | TALKING TO PARENTS | (Harder) |

| Better | SCIENTIFIC THINKING | (Worse) |

| (More) | BEING INFLUENCED BY FRIENDS | Less |

| Easier | GETTING TO SLEEP AT NIGHT | (Harder) |

Chart A.1 An example of a typical completed questionnaire.

This was a good way of gauging the response and allowed me to high-light the topics that we were going to discuss as the lesson proceeded. In particular, I was able to start the students thinking about moods and emotions, about stress and sleep. All three of these topics were central to the lesson I was going to deliver.

As can be seen from Table A.1, the three topics I have mentioned are the ones where the results are clearest: 95% of students indicate that as teenagers they are more stressed, 89% are moodier and 75% say it is harder to get to sleep. These are striking results and are, of

Table A.1 Based on 510 responses from students in Years 9 and 10

Change since you became a teenager			
Finding life stressful	More = 95%	**Memory**	Better = 71%
	Less = 5%		Worse = 29%
Being moody	More = 89%	**Talking to parents**	Harder = 70%
	Less = 11%		Easier = 30%
Getting to sleep at night	Harder = 75%	**Scientific reasoning**	Better = 70%
	Easier = 25%		Worse = 30%
Enjoying things that are a bit risky	More – 73%	**Being influenced by friends**	More = 58%
	Less = 27%		Less = 42%

course, extremely useful in the lesson as they provide a clear illustration of the importance of these topics for young people.

The second value of the Questionnaire is that it provided a means of engaging the students and indicating to them that I was interested in their own experiences. I had always been keen to make this lesson interactive, and the Questionnaire was an exercise that was useful in this respect. The other exercises are to be found on the accompanying website (www.routledge.com/cw/coleman).

In addition to all this, there is a third value in the Change Questionnaire. This is that it opens up the possibility of discussing with students why they are experiencing these changes. I illustrated this at the start of Chapter 8 when describing the response to the stress question. Once I knew that the great majority of students were saying they were more stressed, I could then ask them why this was the case. As I make clear in Chapter 8, students state that the main reason has to do with school.

The amount of discussion with students about the items in the Change Questionnaire will, naturally, depend on the time available. The Questionnaire can be used in many different ways. I know that some schools have extended the material from one lesson into a range of lessons over a week. When this is done, there is no limit to the uses that the Questionnaire can be put. I have had excellent discussions with groups of students about the ease or difficulty of talking to parents and about doing things that are a bit risky or what I mean by improvement in scientific reasoning.

Finally, I should add that the Questionnaire can be used in one-to-one sessions with individual students as an excellent icebreaker. It can also be used outside the school setting, and I have had reports of parents using it at home as a way of improving communication with a teenager. I hope readers will find it a useful tool in whatever work they are doing with young people.

Appendix 2
The workshops

Background

This book came about as a result of work I carried out with colleagues in Hertfordshire in the development of the training programme entitled "My Teen Brain". I have described this process in Chapter 3. The first workshop was designed for practitioners – usually social workers, youth workers and others engaged in direct work with young people. Due to the commissioning process, the workshops were not, initially, advertised directly to schools.

As the workshops were rolled out, however, we gradually had teachers, educational psychologists, school counsellors and others from the education sector asking to attend. This led to an increasing interest from schools, and requests for me to deliver a workshop on the teen brain specifically for teachers. I have described the process of developing such a workshop in Chapter 9.

As the work proceeded, those who attended started to ask why we were not developing something similar for students themselves. The argument was put forward that this knowledge would be of considerable value for young people, and we faced pressure to extend the "My Teen Brain" programme to include a lesson plan for students. This work is described in Chapter 10.

During the course of my work I learnt that a team in Oxford have been developing a workshop for secondary school students as part of the Myriad project. In this workshop students of all ages are invited to take part in an interactive quiz and discussion, aided by a blow-up model of the human brain. A reference to this work will be found at the end of the Appendix.

The last stage of the process involved the development of a workshop for parents of teenagers. I was greatly assisted in this particular element of the work by the enthusiasm of staff from the Early Help service in Bedford Borough. They saw that parents would find this knowledge of great value, and they engaged schools in their area to host such workshops. This work is described in Chapter 11.

Delivery

All these workshops make use of a set of slides, together with instructions for tutors. In Hertfordshire, it was decided that the workshops would be run by myself together with experienced trainers from the organization Family Links. In all the early work we had two trainers working together, and this pattern has continued in all the "My Teen Brain" training. However, as the work extended to schools and parents, it was not always possible to have two trainers, and most of the workshops described in Chapters 9, 10 and 11 I delivered as the sole trainer.

Of course, it has not been possible for me to continue to meet the demand for these workshops, and subsequent work has involved the development of a "Training the Trainers" programme. Such programmes have been run in Hertfordshire, Bedford Borough, Parenting Northern Ireland, and through the charity Charlie Waller.

On the website (www.routledge.com/cw/coleman) the reader will find all the slides that have been used for these three different workshops. I have also provided notes to accompany the slides to make it easier for readers to understand the content of each slide. As far as tutor notes are concerned, these are most comprehensive for the lesson plan for students (Chapter 10). This is because I have run a number of training sessions for teachers wishing to deliver this workshop in their schools. As far as the parents' workshop is concerned, I have incorporated instructions to tutors in the actual slides. These are not particularly detailed but should provide sufficient guidance for any experienced tutor. There are no tutor notes for the slides for the teacher workshop, apart from the notes attached to each slide. In my view, the notes should be sufficient for the delivery of this workshop.

Requirements for trainers

Readers who explore the content of the website may well consider delivering one of these workshops themselves. So, what is required for this to be possible? Clearly, it will not be feasible for me to offer training for anyone wishing to pursue this option. Nonetheless, experienced trainers should be able to make use of the materials I have provided.

I strongly believe that anyone wishing to deliver one of the workshops must have had previous experience of working with the group selected. For example, anyone thinking about offering the workshop for parents should have worked with parent groups previously. I also advise that the trainer read thoroughly around the subject and get to a point where they feel confident about answering a range of questions to do with brain development. There are a number of good books about the teenage brain, most of which have been referenced throughout this book. I would encourage as much reading as possible before any delivery of the workshops or the lesson plan for students.

Considerable sensitivity is required in delivering these materials. The reason for this is that the information is of a general nature and does not deal with particular issues or individual cases. Attendees at workshops may have concerns about their own teenagers or complex topics such as autism, teenage pregnancy or childhood trauma. Trainers need to be conscious of such concerns. If offering a workshop, trainers should make clear at the outset the limits of what is going to be delivered. Trainers should ensure that additional information is made available to support anyone who has particular concerns.

As far as the students are concerned, I have made it clear in Chapter 10 that this lesson was not designed to address issues about mental health. I believe it is important to avoid anything that may raise sensitive personal issues. I have included an exercise on dealing with stress, but I have been careful to keep it at a general level. Of course, any teacher will be aware of the need to be alert to individual students who may find the material difficult. All schools will have support systems in place if this proves necessary. However, these materials have been designed to avoid causing any distress to students.

Delivery on virtual platforms

During 2020 and 2021, I have delivered these workshops through online platforms such as Zoom and Teams. It may be that readers will wish to do the same in the future. Even without the pandemic, we have discovered that there are some advantages to online delivery. This format overcomes any geographical constraints, but it is also good for parents because it avoids childcare issues, reduces travel and makes timing easier. If any reader is planning to deliver a workshop in this manner, my experience has taught me that the following points are important to keep in mind.

- Always have a convenor or facilitator with you to manage the waiting room, the chat room and to deal with any technical issues
- Think carefully about the numbers you want to attend, especially if you plan to use break-out rooms
- Consider how to manage the exercises, since they cannot be undertaken in the same way as you would in a face-to-face workshop;
- Think through how you will manage questions. It may be that you will want to set up a system for participants to get in touch after the workshop if they have unanswered queries
- Lastly, plan to make additional material available for the participants. This should include an introduction to the teenage brain so that they have something to read afterwards, and information about additional support if participants are left with anxieties arising from the workshop.

The future

It will be apparent to readers that I am enthusiastic about the value of learning about teenage brain development. I believe that this can make a considerable difference to both adults and young people. I have written this book so that as wide an audience as possible can learn about this topic. This knowledge can be used to improve the personal development of teenagers and to enable adults and young people to relate to each other more positively. I wish all readers good luck in furthering their knowledge of this fascinating topic.

Reference

The Teenage Brain Resources Pack, MYRIAD project, The University of Oxford Department of Psychiatry http://myriadproject.org/public-engagement/educational-resources/the-teenage-brain/

Index

Page numbers in *italics* represent photographs or figures.

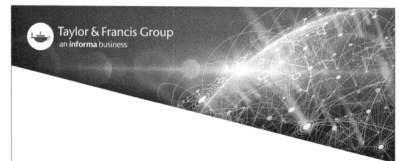

www.ingramcontent.com/pod-product-compliance
Ingram Content Group UK Ltd.
Pitfield, Milton Keynes, MK11 3LW, UK
UKHW020416010325
455677UK00029B/907